Map Mastery: A Beginner's Guide to Easy Map Reading

N.B. Singh

DEDICATION

To Nature,

I dedicate this book to you, the source of all life. You are my inspiration, my teacher, and my friend.

Thank you for teaching me about the beauty of the world around me. Thank you for showing me the power of the natural world. Thank you for giving me a sense of peace and tranquillity.

I promise to do my part to protect you and your many wonders. I will teach my children about the importance of conservation and sustainability. I will work to make the world a better place for all living things.

Thank you for everything, Nature.

With love,

N.B Singh

Contents

PREFACE

Welcome to *Map Mastery: A Beginner's Guide to Easy Map Reading.* In a world filled with maps guiding our journeys, whether in the wilderness or urban landscapes, developing map reading skills is essential. This book is designed to be your companion on the exciting journey of mastering the art and science of map reading.

As a beginner-friendly guide, I aim to make the learning process enjoyable and stress-free. Each section is crafted to provide practical insights, real-world applications, and hands-on exercises. Whether you're navigating with a compass, exploring digital maps, or delving into historical cartography, this book covers it all.

No prior experience is needed; just bring your curiosity and enthusiasm for exploring the world through maps. By the end of this guide, you'll have the confidence to interpret maps, navigate with ease, and even share your newfound knowledge with others.

I hope you find this book not only informative but also a source of inspiration for your adventures. Happy map reading!

N.B. Singh

Chapter 1

Introduction

1.1 Understanding Maps

Maps are powerful tools that help us navigate and comprehend our surroundings. Let's break down the essentials without overwhelming complexity.

1.1.1 Basic Map Components

A map comprises key elements:

- **Scale (S):** The ratio of a distance on the map to the corresponding distance on the ground. Use $S = \dfrac{\text{Map Distance}}{\text{Ground Distance}}$.

- **Legend:** A guide explaining symbols and colors used on the map.

- **Orientation:** Understanding cardinal directions (North, South, East, West).

- **Coordinates:** Latitude and Longitude to pinpoint a location globally.

1.1.2 Coordinate Systems

Latitude and Longitude

Latitude (ϕ) and Longitude (λ) determine a point's position on Earth.

$$\text{Coordinates: } (\phi, \lambda)$$

UTM (Universal Transverse Mercator)

Easting (E), Northing (N) coordinates provide localized accuracy.

1.1.3   Map Reading in Action

Measuring Distances

$$\text{Distance} = \sqrt{(x_2 - x_1)^2 + (y_2 - y_1)^2}$$

Compass Bearings

$$\text{Compass Bearing } (\theta) = \tan^{-1}\left(\frac{\Delta y}{\Delta x}\right)$$

Map Scale Application

$$\text{Ground Distance} = \frac{\text{Map Distance}}{\text{Scale}}$$

Understanding maps is fundamental. No pressure, just practical knowledge to guide your way!

1.2   Importance of Map Reading

Understanding the significance of map reading is key for practical navigation. Let's explore its importance in a swift and memorable manner.

1.2.1   Efficient Route Planning

$$\text{Time} = \frac{\text{Distance}}{\text{Speed}}$$

Map reading allows for optimal route planning, minimizing travel time. Knowing distances and terrains aids in choosing the fastest paths.

1.2.2   Environmental Awareness

$$\text{Environmental Impact} = \frac{\text{Resources Used}}{\text{Distance Traveled}}$$

Map reading fosters eco-friendly choices. Being aware of surroundings helps reduce environmental impact during journeys.

1.2.3 Emergency Preparedness

$$\text{Emergency Response Time} = \frac{\text{Distance}}{\text{Speed}}$$

In emergencies, quick and accurate navigation is crucial. Map reading enhances your ability to respond swiftly to unforeseen situations.

1.2.4 Economic Considerations

$$\text{Cost Efficiency} = \frac{\text{Distance Traveled}}{\text{Fuel Cost}}$$

Efficient map use contributes to cost-effective travel. Understanding distances aids in budget-friendly navigation.

1.2.5 Educational and Cultural Exploration

$$\text{Cultural Heritage} = \frac{\text{Historical Sites Explored}}{\text{Total Sites}}$$

Map reading enriches educational and cultural experiences. Navigating with maps opens doors to historical and cultural exploration.

1.2.6 Global Understanding

$$\text{Global Connectivity} = \frac{\text{Map Interaction}}{\text{Cultural Exchange}}$$

Maps foster global connectivity. Engaging with diverse maps promotes cultural exchange and a broader understanding of the world.

Map reading is more than a skill; it's a gateway to efficiency, awareness, and exploration.

1.3 Basic Map Components

Navigating maps becomes simpler when we grasp the fundamental components swiftly. Let's explore the essentials in a practical and memorable way.

1.3.1 Scale Essentials

$$\text{Scale} = \frac{\text{Map Distance}}{\text{Ground Distance}}$$

Think of the scale as the map's zoom level. The ratio tells you how much the map has shrunk in comparison to the actual terrain.

1.3.2   Cracking the Legend Code

The legend is your map's secret language. It decodes symbols, colors, and markings. It's like the map's own unique dictionary.

1.3.3   Orient Yourself

Understanding cardinal directions is like having a built-in compass. North, South, East, West - your basic compass rose is your guide.

1.3.4   Coordinates Demystified

$$\text{Coordinates: } (\text{Latitude}, \text{Longitude})$$

Think of coordinates as the map's GPS. They pinpoint locations globally, allowing precise navigation.

1.3.5   Grid Power: UTM Coordinates

$$\text{Easting (E)}, \text{Northing (N)}$$

UTM coordinates provide localized accuracy. Imagine the map as a giant grid, and UTM tells you exactly where you are on that grid.

1.3.6   Map Reading 101: Putting It All Together

$$\text{Ground Distance} = \frac{\text{Map Distance}}{\text{Scale}}$$

Map reading is like solving a puzzle. Connect the pieces – scale, legend, orientation, coordinates, and grids – to reveal your route.

Understanding maps is your key to unlocking new territories effortlessly.

1.4   Tools for Map Navigation

Equip yourself with the right tools for seamless map navigation. Let's dive into practical and memorable insights without the mental pressure.

1.4.1 Compass Magic

$$\text{Compass Bearing } (\theta) = \tan^{-1}\left(\frac{\Delta y}{\Delta x}\right)$$

Think of a compass as your map's best friend. It points you in the right direction, helping you stay on course.

1.4.2 Rulers and Protractors: Measure Like a Pro

$$\text{Distance} = \sqrt{(x_2 - x_1)^2 + (y_2 - y_1)^2}$$

Rulers and protractors are your map's measuring tape. Measure distances accurately for effective route planning.

1.4.3 GPS: Your Digital Navigator

$$\text{GPS Accuracy} = \frac{\text{Reported Distance}}{\text{Actual Distance}} \times 100$$

GPS turns your map into a digital guide. Understand its accuracy to trust your digital navigation companion.

1.4.4 Altimeter: Navigating Heights

$$\text{Height Gain or Loss} = \text{Final Altitude} - \text{Initial Altitude}$$

An altimeter tells you about the highs and lows. Navigate terrain by tracking changes in altitude.

1.4.5 Map Case and Protection

A map case is like armor for your map. Keep it dry and protected to ensure clarity and longevity during your journey.

1.4.6 Binoculars: Zooming In

$$\text{Field of View } (FOV) = \frac{\text{Width of Area Visible}}{\text{Distance from Viewer}}$$

Binoculars enhance your map-reading experience. Calculate the field of view to understand your visual scope.

Arm yourself with these tools, and map navigation becomes an adventure, not a challenge.

1.5 Key Terms in Map Reading

Unlock the language of maps effortlessly by diving into key terms. Let's explore these terms in a way that sticks, without the mental pressure.

1.5.1 Scale Unveiled

$$\text{Scale} = \frac{\text{Map Distance}}{\text{Ground Distance}}$$

Think of the scale as a map's magnifying glass. It shows you how much the map has zoomed in or out compared to the real world.

1.5.2 Legend Decoded

The legend is like a map's secret code. It interprets symbols, colors, and markings, guiding you through the map's language.

1.5.3 Cardinal Directions: Navigational Anchors

North, South, East, West - cardinal directions are your navigational anchors. Orient yourself by understanding these basic points.

1.5.4 Coordinates Demystified

$$\text{Coordinates: } (\text{Latitude}, \text{Longitude})$$

Coordinates act as your map's GPS coordinates. They pinpoint locations globally, allowing for precise navigation.

1.5.5 Elevation Essentials

$$\text{Elevation Gain or Loss} = \text{Final Elevation} - \text{Initial Elevation}$$

Elevation changes are like the map's hills and valleys. Understand elevation to navigate different terrains effectively.

1.5.6 Contours: Reading the Landscape

Contours are like the topographic wrinkles on a map. They depict changes in elevation. The closer they are, the steeper the terrain.

Mastering these key terms transforms map reading into a fluent conversation with your surroundings.

1.6 Getting Started with Maps

Embark on your map-reading journey seamlessly. Let's jump into the basics without the mental pressure, making it both fun and practical.

1.6.1 Map Unfolding Magic

$$\text{Map Area} = \pi r^2$$

Unfold your map like unwrapping a gift. The larger the area, the more details you'll discover. Embrace the unfolding magic!

1.6.2 Orientation Hacks

$$\text{Orientation Angle } (\alpha) = \tan^{-1}\left(\frac{\text{Opposite Side}}{\text{Adjacent Side}}\right)$$

Think of map orientation like finding your way with a compass. Calculate angles to stay on the right path.

1.6.3 Map Symbols: The Language of Icons

Symbols on maps are like emojis for navigation. Decode them to understand landmarks, terrain, and features effortlessly.

1.6.4 Simple Distance Estimation

$$\text{Estimated Distance} = \text{Pace} \times \text{Number of Paces}$$

Estimate distances with your natural pace. It's like measuring with your own footsteps – simple and effective.

1.6.5 Choosing the Right Map

$$\text{Map Suitability} = \frac{\text{Scale}}{\text{Map Area}}$$

Choosing the right map is like selecting the right tool for the job. Consider both scale and map area for effective navigation.

1.6.6 Starting with Simple Coordinates

$$\text{Coordinates: } (\text{Latitude}, \text{Longitude})$$

Kickstart your journey by understanding basic coordinates. It's like learning the address of your destination.

Getting started with maps is an adventure in itself. Enjoy the process, and let the maps guide your way!

Chapter 2

Getting to Know Maps

2.1 Types of Maps

Explore the world of maps effortlessly by delving into the different types. Let's navigate through the variety without the mental pressure.

2.1.1 Topographic Maps: Elevations Unveiled

$$\text{Contour Interval} = \frac{\text{Total Elevation Range}}{\text{Number of Contour Lines}}$$

Topographic maps are like 3D puzzles. Contour lines reveal elevation changes. The closer they are, the steeper the terrain.

2.1.2 Political Maps: Borders and Boundaries

Political maps are like the world's ID. They outline countries, states, and regions, simplifying the understanding of political boundaries.

2.1.3 Physical Maps: Landforms Illustrated

Physical maps are Earth's portraits. They showcase mountains, rivers, and deserts, giving a visual overview of the planet's features.

2.1.4   Climate Maps: Weather Visualized

Climate maps are like meteorological snapshots. They illustrate temperature, precipitation, and climate zones, making weather patterns clear.

2.1.5   Navigation Charts: Nautical Navigations

$$\text{Speed} = \frac{\text{Distance}}{\text{Time}}$$

Navigation charts are sailors' guides. Use speed calculations to plan efficient routes and sail smoothly.

2.1.6   Mind Maps: Creative Exploration

Mind maps are your mental canvas. They organize thoughts visually, creating interconnected branches for effective brainstorming.

Discovering map types is like finding the right tool for different tasks. Each map serves a unique purpose in your exploration journey.

2.2   Scale and Projections

Dive into the world of scales and projections without the mental pressure. Let's understand these map essentials in a swift and memorable way.

2.2.1   Scale Magic: Shrinking and Enlarging

$$\text{Scale} = \frac{\text{Map Distance}}{\text{Ground Distance}}$$

Scale is like a map's magnifying glass. The ratio reveals how much the map has zoomed in or out compared to the actual terrain.

2.2.2   Choosing the Right Scale

$$\text{Map Suitability} = \frac{\text{Scale}}{\text{Map Area}}$$

Selecting the right scale is crucial. Balance both scale and map area for effective navigation and detailed exploration.

2.2.3 Mercator Projection: Straightforward Navigation

Mercator projection is like stretching a globe onto paper. It preserves angles, making it ideal for navigation but distorts sizes at extreme latitudes.

2.2.4 Conic Projection: Regional Realism

Conic projection is like wrapping paper around a cone. It maintains accurate land shapes in a specific region, ideal for mapping smaller areas.

2.2.5 Cylindrical Projection: Global Views

Cylindrical projection is like rolling a globe onto paper. It preserves equatorial areas but distorts shapes toward the poles, suitable for world maps.

2.2.6 Understanding Distortion: Trade-offs in Mapmaking

$$\text{Distortion} = \frac{\text{Change in Size}}{\text{Original Size}} \times 100$$

Distortion is the mapmaker's challenge. Understand trade-offs in size, shape, and distance when choosing projections.

Navigating scales and projections is like choosing the right lens for your map camera. Each has its purpose, and understanding them enhances your map-reading skills.

2.3 Legend and Symbols

Decode the language of maps effortlessly with insights into legends and symbols. Let's unravel the symbols without the mental pressure.

2.3.1 Legend Magic: Your Map's Dictionary

The legend is like a map's dictionary. It decodes symbols, colors, and markings, guiding you through the map's language.

2.3.2 Color Codes: Vibrant Navigation

Colors on maps are like traffic signals. They convey information quickly. Memorize color codes for swift navigation.

2.3.3 Line Symbols: Pathways Revealed

$$\text{Distance} = \sqrt{(x_2 - x_1)^2 + (y_2 - y_1)^2}$$

Line symbols on maps represent pathways. Use the distance formula to estimate travel distances between points.

2.3.4 Point Symbols: Landmarks Unveiled

Point symbols mark landmarks. Identify them like a traveler spotting familiar places. They serve as reference points.

2.3.5 Area Symbols: Regions Defined

Area symbols highlight regions. Imagine them as colored patches on your map, defining territories and zones.

2.3.6 Understanding Map Symbols in Action

$$\text{Map Interpretation} = \text{Legend} + \text{Symbols} + \text{Context}$$

Interpreting maps is like solving a puzzle. Combine the legend, symbols, and context for a clear understanding.

Navigating legends and symbols is like learning a new alphabet. Once mastered, they open up a world of map reading with ease.

2.4 Grids and Coordinates

Unlock the power of grids and coordinates effortlessly. Let's dive into these map essentials in a swift and memorable way.

2.4.1   Grid Basics: Like a Graph on Your Map

Imagine the map as a giant graph paper. The grid divides it into manageable squares, simplifying location identification.

2.4.2   UTM Coordinates: Precision in Positioning

$$\text{Easting (E)}, \text{Northing (N)}$$

UTM coordinates act like a GPS for localized accuracy. Think of them as pinpointing your location on a grid.

2.4.3   Latitude and Longitude: Global GPS Coordinates

$$\text{Coordinates: (Latitude}, \text{Longitude)}$$

Latitude and Longitude are like the global coordinates of your map. They pinpoint locations globally for precise navigation.

2.4.4   Grid Navigation: Plotting Your Course

$$\text{Distance} = \sqrt{(x_2 - x_1)^2 + (y_2 - y_1)^2}$$

Navigating on a grid is like plotting points on a graph. Use the distance formula to calculate distances between grid points.

2.4.5   Magnetic Declination: True vs. Magnetic North

$$\text{True Bearing} = \text{Magnetic Bearing} + \text{Magnetic Declination}$$

Magnetic declination is like a compass adjustment. Correct your magnetic bearings for more accurate navigation.

2.4.6   Practical Map Grid Use

$$\text{Grid Coordinates} = \text{Grid Reference} + \text{Subdivisions}$$

Use grid coordinates like a map's address. Combine grid references and subdivisions for precise location identification.

Mastering grids and coordinates is like learning the coordinates of your map's treasure. They guide you to your destination with precision.

2.5 Reading Topographic Maps

Embark on the journey of reading topographic maps with ease. Let's navigate through the contours and features without the mental pressure.

2.5.1 Contour Lines: 3D Maps on Paper

Contour lines are like the elevation wrinkles of your map. The closer they are, the steeper the terrain. Imagine them as 3D maps on paper.

2.5.2 Contour Interval: Decoding Elevation Changes

$$\text{Contour Interval} = \frac{\text{Total Elevation Range}}{\text{Number of Contour Lines}}$$

Contour intervals reveal elevation changes. The smaller the interval, the finer the details on your topographic map.

2.5.3 Identifying Hills and Valleys

$$\text{Hill or Ridge} = \text{Contours Closing In}$$

Contours closing in on a topographic map indicate hills or ridges. Think of them as the peaks on your map.

$$\text{Valley} = \text{Contours Spreading Out}$$

Contours spreading out on a topographic map indicate valleys. Visualize them as the low points between hills.

2.5.4 Understanding Depression Contours

Depression contours are like the map's valleys within valleys. They indicate lower points, such as sinkholes or basins.

2.5.5 Slope Calculation: Steepness Revealed

$$\text{Slope Percentage} = \tan(\alpha) \times 100$$

Calculate slope percentage to gauge steepness. A higher percentage means a steeper slope on your topographic map.

2.5.6 Using Topographic Maps for Navigation

$$\text{Route Planning} = \text{Understanding Contour Patterns}$$

Plan routes on a topographic map by interpreting contour patterns. Follow the lines for smooth and efficient navigation.

Reading topographic maps is like unraveling nature's secrets on paper. Contours become your guide, revealing the landscape effortlessly.

2.6 Digital vs. Paper Maps

Explore the realm of maps in both digital and paper forms effortlessly. Let's compare the pros and cons without any mental pressure.

2.6.1 Digital Maps: Navigating with Technology

Digital maps are like your pocket-sized guides. They offer dynamic features, real-time updates, and interactive navigation.

$$\text{Accuracy of Digital Maps} = \frac{\text{Correct Position Reports}}{\text{Total Position Reports}} \times 100$$

Digital maps provide accurate positions with the ratio of correct position reports to the total.

2.6.2 Paper Maps: Tangible Explorations

Paper maps are your traditional companions. They offer a tangible experience, a big-picture view, and no dependency on technology.

$$\text{Ease of Use of Paper Maps} = \frac{\text{Successful Navigation Attempts}}{\text{Total Navigation Attempts}} \times 100$$

Paper maps are user-friendly with successful navigation attempts as a percentage of total attempts.

2.6.3 Battery Life: A Digital Consideration

$$\text{Effective Battery Life} = \frac{\text{Actual Usage Time}}{\text{Advertised Battery Life}} \times 100$$

For digital maps, effective battery life is crucial. It's the ratio of actual usage time to the advertised battery life.

2.6.4   Environmental Impact: A Paper Consideration

$$\text{Carbon Footprint} = \frac{\text{Paper Production Emissions}}{\text{Total Emissions}} \times 100$$

Consider the environmental impact of paper maps. Calculate the carbon footprint as the ratio of paper production emissions to total emissions.

2.6.5   Map Choice: Finding Your Preference

$$\text{Map Preference Index} = \text{Digital Benefits} - \text{Paper Benefits}$$

Choose your map preference based on a personalized index considering the benefits of both digital and paper maps.

Choosing between digital and paper maps is like selecting tools for a job. Consider your needs, preferences, and the nature of your exploration for an optimized map experience.

Chapter 3

Compass Navigation

3.1 Introduction to Compass Use

Embark on the journey of compass navigation with simplicity and practical insights. Let's explore the basics without any mental pressure.

3.1.1 Compass Anatomy: Your Navigational Tool

A compass consists of a magnetic needle pointing to the magnetic north. Orient yourself by aligning the needle with the compass housing.

3.1.2 Understanding Cardinal Directions

$$\text{Compass Bearing } (\theta) = \tan^{-1}\left(\frac{\Delta y}{\Delta x}\right)$$

Cardinal directions - North, South, East, West - are your navigational anchors. Calculate compass bearing using the tangent formula.

3.1.3 Declination Adjustment: True vs. Magnetic North

$$\text{True Bearing} = \text{Magnetic Bearing} + \text{Magnetic Declination}$$

Adjust for magnetic declination to convert magnetic bearing to true bearing for accurate navigation.

3.1.4   Using the Compass for Land Navigation

$$\text{Distance} = \sqrt{(x_2 - x_1)^2 + (y_2 - y_1)^2}$$

Navigate on land using the compass for direction and distance. Apply the distance formula to estimate travel distances.

3.1.5   Navigating with Map and Compass Together

$$\text{Route Planning} = \text{Understanding Contour Patterns}$$

Combine map and compass for effective navigation. Plan routes by interpreting contour patterns on topographic maps.

3.1.6   Emergency Navigation Techniques

In emergencies, use the compass for basic navigation. Follow a straight-line direction to reach a known point or safety.

Compass navigation is like having a reliable friend in the wild. Master its basics for confident and accurate navigation on your journeys.

3.2   Types of Compasses

Explore the world of compasses effortlessly by understanding the types in a quick and memorable way.

3.2.1   Baseplate Compass: Your Compact Guide

A baseplate compass is like your pocket guide. It includes a transparent baseplate with a ruler and scales for map measurements.

3.2.2   Lensatic Compass: Precision in Sight

A lensatic compass is your precision tool. It uses a sighting lens for accurate readings, perfect for advanced navigation.

3.2.3 Orienteering Compass: Swift and Simple

An orienteering compass is your swift companion. It features a transparent baseplate and a rotating dial, ideal for quick navigation.

3.2.4 Digital Compass: Technology in Your Hand

A digital compass is like a tech-savvy guide. It provides precise digital readings, often combined with other features for enhanced navigation.

3.2.5 Floating Compass: Liquid Stability

A floating compass ensures stability. The needle floats in liquid, minimizing friction for smoother and more accurate readings.

3.2.6 Wrist Compass: On-the-Go Navigation

A wrist compass is like wearing navigation on your sleeve. It's compact, hands-free, and perfect for quick, on-the-go reference.

3.2.7 Practical Considerations in Compass Choice

$$\text{Compass Suitability Index} = \text{Digital Features} - \text{Traditional Benefits}$$

Select your compass based on personal preference. Calculate the Compass Suitability Index by comparing digital features to traditional benefits.

Choosing a compass is like picking the right tool for the job. Consider your navigation needs and preferences to find the perfect compass companion.

3.3 Orienting a Map with a Compass

Master the art of orienting a map with a compass effortlessly. Let's align your map like a pro without any mental pressure.

3.3.1 Aligning Map and Compass: The Basics

To align your map with a compass, place the compass on the map with the direction of travel arrow pointing towards your destination.

3.3.2 Setting the Declination: True North vs. Magnetic North

$$\text{True Bearing} = \text{Magnetic Bearing} + \text{Magnetic Declination}$$

Adjust for magnetic declination by adding or subtracting it from your magnetic bearing to get the true bearing.

3.3.3 Using a Compass to Find True North

Hold the compass level and turn yourself until the magnetic needle aligns with the orienting arrow. Your body now faces true north.

3.3.4 Orienting a Map with Known Landmarks

$$\text{Angle to Landmark} = \tan^{-1}\left(\frac{\text{Height of Landmark}}{\text{Distance to Landmark}}\right)$$

Orient your map using known landmarks. Calculate the angle to a landmark using the tangent formula for precise alignment.

3.3.5 Orienting with Sun or Stars: Celestial Navigation

In the absence of a compass, use the sun or stars. The sun rises in the east and sets in the west, aiding in basic orientation.

$$\text{Star Declination} = \text{Observer's Latitude} + (\text{Star's Altitude} - 90°)$$

For stars, calculate their declination to determine north based on your observer's latitude.

3.3.6 Quick Map Orientation Tips

Remember the acronym "MNEMONIC": - M: Map on ground - N: Needle points north - E: Edge aligns with east

Orienting a map is like aligning pieces of a puzzle. Use your compass to connect the map with the real world effortlessly.

3.4 Following Bearings

Navigate with ease by following bearings like a pro. Let's break it down without any mental pressure.

3.4.1 Setting Your Bearing: The Starting Point

To set a bearing, rotate the compass housing until your desired direction of travel aligns with the direction of travel arrow.

3.4.2 Pacing: Measuring Distances on Foot

$$\text{Estimated Distance} = \text{Pace} \times \text{Number of Paces}$$

Measure distances on foot using pacing. Estimate distances by multiplying your pace length by the number of paces.

3.4.3 Dead Reckoning: Calculating Your Position

Use dead reckoning to estimate your current position. Start from a known point, follow bearings, and calculate distances traveled.

$$\text{Final Position} = \text{Initial Position} + \text{Distance Traveled}$$

3.4.4 Back Bearings: Navigating Backwards

$$\text{Back Bearing} = \text{Forward Bearing} + 180°$$

Navigate backward by adding 180 degrees to your forward bearing. It helps when retracing your steps or correcting course.

3.4.5 Triangulation: Pinpointing Your Location

$$\text{Triangulation Point} = \frac{a + b + c}{3}$$

Use triangulation to pinpoint your location. Measure bearings to a landmark from different positions and find the average.

3.4.6   Resection: Finding Your Position

$$\text{Resection Point} = \frac{a \times x_a + b \times x_b + c \times x_c}{a + b + c}$$

Use resection to find your position. Measure bearings to known landmarks and calculate your location based on those angles.

Following bearings is like creating your own path through the wilderness. Master these techniques for confident and accurate navigation on your adventures.

3.5   Navigating with a Compass

Navigate through the wild with confidence using your compass. Let's simplify the process without any mental pressure.

3.5.1   Setting Your Course: The Starting Point

Set your course by aligning your compass with your destination. The direction of travel arrow guides your way.

3.5.2   Measuring Distances On Foot

$$\text{Estimated Distance} = \text{Pace} \times \text{Number of Paces}$$

Measure distances on foot using pacing. Estimate distances by multiplying your pace length by the number of paces.

3.5.3   Using Landmarks as Checkpoints

Landmarks are your navigational checkpoints. Identify distinct features and use them to confirm your position along the route.

3.5.4   Adjusting for Declination: True vs. Magnetic North

$$\text{True Bearing} = \text{Magnetic Bearing} + \text{Magnetic Declination}$$

Adjust for magnetic declination to convert magnetic bearing to true bearing for accurate navigation.

3.5.5 Checking Bearings Along the Way

Periodically check your compass bearing along the way. Ensure you are on course and make adjustments if needed.

3.5.6 Taking Back Bearings for Verification

$$\text{Back Bearing} = \text{Forward Bearing} + 180°$$

Verify your course by taking back bearings. Add 180 degrees to your forward bearing and compare it with your starting point.

3.5.7 Emergency Techniques: Lost but Not Helpless

In emergencies, use basic techniques. Follow a straight line or retrace your steps using the compass for basic navigation.

Navigating with a compass is like dancing through nature's pathways. Trust your compass, stay aware, and enjoy the adventure with confidence.

3.6 Common Compass Mistakes

Avoid the pitfalls of compass navigation by steering clear of these common mistakes. Let's navigate through them with ease.

3.6.1 Misalignment with True North

$$\text{True Bearing} = \text{Magnetic Bearing} + \text{Magnetic Declination}$$

Misalignment occurs when not adjusting for magnetic declination. Ensure your compass points to true north for accurate navigation.

3.6.2 Ignoring Pace Variability

$$\text{Estimated Distance} = \text{Pace} \times \text{Number of Paces}$$

Ignoring pace variability leads to distance miscalculations. Be aware that your pace may vary, affecting estimated distances.

3.6.3 Overlooking Landmark Variations

$$\text{Triangulation Point} = \frac{a + b + c}{3}$$

Overlooking variations in landmark appearances affects triangulation accuracy. Consider multiple viewpoints for better triangulation.

3.6.4 Neglecting Back Bearings for Verification

$$\text{Back Bearing} = \text{Forward Bearing} + 180°$$

Neglecting back bearings leaves your route unverified. Always take back bearings to confirm your path.

3.6.5 Forgetting to Reorient After Deviations

After deviations, forgetting to reorient your map leads to incorrect navigation. Always realign your map and compass for accurate readings.

3.6.6 Failure to Consider Magnetic Declination Changes

$$\text{Declination Change Rate} = \frac{\text{Change in Declination}}{\text{Change in Time}}$$

Failure to consider changes in magnetic declination over time impacts navigation accuracy. Be aware of declination change rates.

3.6.7 Relying Solely on Technology

$$\text{Compass Suitability Index} = \text{Digital Features} - \text{Traditional Benefits}$$

Relying solely on technology without a backup plan can lead to navigation failures. Consider a compass suitability index for balanced navigation.

Navigating with a compass is an art, and avoiding these common mistakes is your brushstroke for accurate and confident exploration.

Chapter 4

Land Navigation Techniques

4.1 Using Landmarks

Unlock the secrets of navigation by mastering the art of using landmarks. Let's explore this technique effortlessly.

4.1.1 Landmark Identification: Nature's Fingerprint

$$\text{Landmark Identification Index} = \frac{\text{Unique Features}}{\text{Total Features}} \times 100$$

Efficient navigation starts with recognizing unique terrain features. Calculate the Landmark Identification Index by dividing unique features by total features and multiplying by 100.

4.1.2 Distance Estimation with Landmarks

$$\text{Distance to Landmark} = \frac{\text{Height of Landmark}}{\tan(\alpha)}$$

Estimate distances to landmarks using their height and the angle (α) of inclination. The tangent formula helps calculate the distance.

4.1.3 Using Landmarks for Route Planning

$$\text{Route Adjustment} = \frac{\text{Distance to Landmark}}{\text{Total Distance}} \times 100$$

Landmarks guide your route. Adjust your course by calculating the route adjustment percentage based on the distance to a landmark and the total distance.

4.1.4 Precision Navigation with Landmarks

$$\text{Attack Point Distance} = \text{Distance to Target} \times \text{Accuracy Percentage}$$

Navigate with precision using attack points. Calculate the distance to an attack point by multiplying the target distance by the desired accuracy percentage.

4.1.5 Identifying Landmarks at Night

Night navigation is possible with stars and celestial landmarks. Identify constellations and use their positions for orientation.

4.1.6 Landmarks in Emergency Navigation

In emergencies, landmarks become lifelines. Identify prominent features and use them to navigate back to safety.

Using landmarks is like reading nature's map. Let them be your guide, and navigation becomes a journey of discovery and exploration.

4.2 Dead Reckoning

Navigate confidently with dead reckoning – a technique that keeps you on track without the mental pressure.

4.2.1 Setting Your Course: The Starting Point

To begin dead reckoning, set your course by identifying a visible landmark or point in the distance.

4.2.2 Measuring Distance Traveled

$$\text{Estimated Distance} = \text{Pace} \times \text{Number of Paces}$$

Measure distances on foot using pacing. Estimate distances by multiplying your pace length by the number of paces.

4.2.3 Calculating Speed and Time

$$\text{Speed} = \frac{\text{Distance Traveled}}{\text{Time Taken}}$$

Calculate your walking speed by dividing the distance traveled by the time taken. This helps in estimating the time needed for your journey.

4.2.4 Estimating Time of Arrival

$$\text{Time of Arrival} = \text{Current Time} + \frac{\text{Remaining Distance}}{\text{Average Speed}}$$

Estimate your time of arrival by adding the remaining distance divided by your average speed to the current time.

4.2.5 Updating Your Position

$$\text{Final Position} = \text{Initial Position} + \text{Distance Traveled}$$

Update your position by adding the distance traveled to your initial position. This gives you an estimate of your final location.

4.2.6 Navigating Around Obstacles

Incorporate dead reckoning around obstacles. Adjust your course and distance based on the terrain, keeping your destination in sight.

4.2.7 Emergency Use of Dead Reckoning

In emergencies, dead reckoning becomes a crucial tool. Follow a straight-line course based on your initial direction for a safe route.

Dead reckoning is like your navigation companion, always guiding you forward. Master this technique, and your journeys become precise and purposeful.

4.3 Pacing and Estimation

Navigate the wild with confidence using the simplicity of pacing and estimation. Let's break it down without any mental pressure.

4.3.1 Pacing: Measuring Distances on Foot

$$\text{Estimated Distance} = \text{Pace} \times \text{Number of Paces}$$

Measure distances on foot using pacing. Estimate distances by multiplying your pace length by the number of paces.

4.3.2 Calibrating Your Pacing

$$\text{Calibrated Pace Length} = \frac{\text{Known Distance}}{\text{Number of Paces}}$$

Calibrate your pacing by measuring a known distance and dividing it by the number of paces. This gives you a calibrated pace length.

4.3.3 Estimating Distance with Known Pacing

$$\text{Estimated Distance} = \text{Calibrated Pace Length} \times \text{Number of Paces}$$

Estimate distances using your calibrated pace length. Multiply it by the number of paces to get the estimated distance.

4.3.4 Time and Speed Estimation

$$\text{Speed} = \frac{\text{Distance}}{\text{Time}}$$

Estimate your walking speed by dividing the distance traveled by the time taken. This helps in pacing calculations.

$$\text{Estimated Time of Arrival} = \frac{\text{Estimated Distance}}{\text{Average Speed}}$$

Estimate your time of arrival by dividing the estimated distance by your average walking speed.

4.3.5 Pacing with Terrain Variations

Adjust your pacing for different terrains. Shorten your pace on uphill climbs and lengthen it on downhill descents for more accurate estimations.

4.3.6 Emergency Pacing Techniques

In emergencies, use pacing for basic navigation. Follow a straight-line course based on your initial direction and pace count.

Pacing and estimation are your trusty companions in the wilderness. Master these techniques, and your journeys become a rhythmic and confident exploration.

4.4 Route Planning

Embark on your journey with effective route planning – a straightforward process without any mental pressure.

4.4.1 Identifying Key Landmarks

$$\text{Landmark Identification Index} = \frac{\text{Unique Features}}{\text{Total Features}} \times 100$$

Start your route planning by identifying key landmarks. Calculate the Landmark Identification Index to recognize unique terrain features.

4.4.2 Selecting Checkpoints for Navigation

$$\text{Checkpoint Distance} = \text{Distance to Feature} + \text{Feature Length}$$

Choose checkpoints strategically for navigation. Calculate the checkpoint distance by adding the distance to a feature and its length.

4.4.3 Utilizing Handrailing Techniques

$$\text{Handrailing Distance} = \text{Distance to Feature} + \text{Feature Length}$$

Stay on course using handrailing. Calculate the handrailing distance by adding the distance to a feature and its length.

4.4.4 Dead Reckoning for Linear Routes

$$\text{Final Position} = \text{Initial Position} + \text{Distance Traveled}$$

Plan linear routes with dead reckoning. Update your position by adding the distance traveled to your initial position.

4.4.5   Creating Box Patterns for Exploration

$$\text{Boxing Distance} = 4 \times \text{Side Length}$$

Explore an area systematically with boxing. Calculate the boxing distance by multiplying the side length by four for a square pattern.

4.4.6   Adjusting Routes for Terrain Variations

$$\text{Route Adjustment} = \frac{\text{Distance to Landmark}}{\text{Total Distance}} \times 100$$

Adapt your route for varying terrains. Adjust your course by calculating the route adjustment percentage based on the distance to a landmark and the total distance.

Route planning is like crafting your adventure. Use these techniques for precise and purposeful journeys through the wilderness.

4.5   Terrain Association

Master the art of navigation through terrain association – a straightforward approach without any mental pressure.

4.5.1   Landmark Identification: Nature's Fingerprint

$$\text{Landmark Identification Index} = \frac{\text{Unique Features}}{\text{Total Features}} \times 100$$

Efficient navigation starts with recognizing unique terrain features. Calculate the Landmark Identification Index by dividing unique features by total features and multiplying by 100.

4.5.2   Using Handrailing Techniques

$$\text{Handrailing Distance} = \text{Distance to Feature} + \text{Feature Length}$$

Stay on course with handrailing. Calculate the handrailing distance by adding the distance to a feature and its length.

4.5.3 Dead Reckoning for Linear Routes

$$\text{Final Position} = \text{Initial Position} + \text{Distance Traveled}$$

Plan linear routes with dead reckoning. Update your position by adding the distance traveled to your initial position.

4.5.4 Attack Points for Precision Navigation

$$\text{Attack Point Distance} = \text{Distance to Target} \times \text{Accuracy Percentage}$$

Navigate precisely with attack points. Calculate the distance to an attack point by multiplying the target distance by the desired accuracy percentage.

4.5.5 Boxing Patterns for Strategic Exploration

$$\text{Boxing Distance} = 4 \times \text{Side Length}$$

Explore an area strategically with boxing. Calculate the boxing distance by multiplying the side length by four for a square pattern.

4.5.6 Steering Through Terrain Variations

$$\text{Steering Angle} = \tan^{-1}\left(\frac{\text{Desired Direction}}{\text{Current Direction}}\right)$$

Navigate naturally with terrain steering. Calculate the steering angle based on your desired and current directions.

Terrain association is like reading nature's map. Let the terrain guide you, and navigation becomes a journey of exploration and discovery.

4.6 Night Navigation

Master the art of navigating in the dark with confidence – a streamlined approach without any mental pressure.

4.6.1   Navigating by Stars

Identify constellations for orientation. The North Star (Polaris) is a reliable guide, always pointing north.

$$\text{Star Declination} = \text{Observer's Latitude} + (\text{Star's Altitude} - 90°)$$

For stars, calculate their declination to determine north based on your observer's latitude.

4.6.2   Using Celestial Bodies

The moon and planets can be used for orientation. Their movement can help indicate direction.

$$\text{Celestial Body Declination} = \text{Observer's Latitude} + (\text{Body's Altitude} - 90°)$$

Calculate the celestial body's declination to find north based on your observer's latitude.

4.6.3   Using Light Sources

Utilize artificial lights for short-range navigation. Be cautious about preserving night vision.

$$\text{Light Bearing} = \tan^{-1}\left(\frac{\text{Distance to Light}}{\text{Height of Light Source}}\right)$$

Determine the direction of a light source using the tangent formula for precise navigation.

4.6.4   Navigation with a Flashlight

Employ a flashlight with a red filter for minimal disruption to night vision. Use it for short-range tasks.

$$\text{Flashlight Range} = \sqrt{2 \times \text{Height of Light Source}}$$

Estimate the range of a flashlight based on the height of the light source.

4.6.5   Using Luminous Compasses

Luminous compasses provide visibility in the dark. Ensure your compass has luminous markings for night use.

$$\text{Compass Bearing at Night} = \text{Magnetic Bearing} + \text{Magnetic Declination}$$

Adjust for magnetic declination to get the true bearing for accurate night navigation.

Night navigation is like unveiling the mysteries of the dark. Let celestial bodies and artificial lights be your guides, and your journey becomes a magical exploration.

Chapter 5

GPS Navigation Basics

5.1 Introduction to GPS

Embark on the world of GPS navigation with ease – a simplified approach without any mental pressure.

5.1.1 Understanding GPS Signals

GPS relies on signals from satellites. The formula for signal travel time is:

$$\text{Signal Travel Time} = \frac{\text{Distance}}{\text{Speed of Light}}$$

Calculate the time taken for signals to travel from satellites to your GPS device.

5.1.2 Triangulation for Positioning

GPS determines your position through triangulation. The formula is:

$$\text{Receiver Position} = \text{Intersection of Satellite Signals}$$

Triangulate your position by intersecting signals from multiple satellites received by your GPS device.

5.1.3   Calculating Distance with GPS

$$\text{Distance} = \text{Speed} \times \text{Time}$$

Calculate your distance traveled by multiplying your speed by the time elapsed, using GPS data.

5.1.4   Speed Estimation with GPS

$$\text{Speed} = \frac{\text{Distance}}{\text{Time}}$$

Estimate your speed using GPS data by dividing the distance traveled by the time elapsed.

5.1.5   Altitude Measurement with GPS

GPS provides altitude information. The formula for altitude is:

$$\text{Altitude} = \text{GPS Altitude} - \text{Geoid Height}$$

Determine your true altitude by subtracting the geoid height from the GPS altitude.

5.1.6   Accuracy and Error in GPS

GPS accuracy is influenced by factors like satellite geometry. The formula for GPS error is:

$$\text{GPS Error} = \text{User Range Error} + \text{Satellite Geometry Error}$$

Understand the factors affecting GPS accuracy and potential errors.

5.1.7   Choosing GPS Units

Consider factors like accuracy, battery life, and features when selecting a GPS unit for your navigation needs.

GPS navigation is like having a personal guide in your pocket. Understanding its basics ensures precise and effortless exploration.

5.2   Understanding GPS Coordinates

Unlock the secrets of GPS coordinates effortlessly – a simplified approach without any mental pressure.

5.2.1 Latitude and Longitude Basics

GPS coordinates are in the form of latitude and longitude. Latitude represents north-south positions, and longitude represents east-west positions.

$$\text{Coordinate Format: Latitude} \pm \text{Longitude}$$

Understand the coordinate format where latitude is represented in degrees north (+) or south (-), and longitude is represented in degrees east (+) or west (-).

5.2.2 Decimal Degrees Format

$$\text{Decimal Degrees} = \text{Degrees} + \left(\frac{\text{Minutes}}{60}\right) + \left(\frac{\text{Seconds}}{3600}\right)$$

Convert traditional degrees, minutes, and seconds to decimal degrees for ease of use in GPS coordinates.

5.2.3 UTM Coordinates

Universal Transverse Mercator (UTM) coordinates provide a two-dimensional Cartesian representation. The format is:

$$\text{UTM: Zone} \pm \text{Eastings} \pm \text{Northings}$$

Understand the UTM format with zones, eastings, and northings for precise positioning.

5.2.4 Converting Coordinates

Use conversion formulas for different coordinate formats. For example, converting decimal degrees to UTM:

$$\text{UTM Eastings} = \text{Earth Radius} \times (\text{Longitude} - \text{Central Meridian})$$

$$\text{UTM Northings} = \text{Earth Radius} \times \ln\left[\tan\left(\frac{\pi}{4} + \frac{\text{Latitude}}{2}\right)\right]$$

Explore the formulas to convert between coordinate systems based on your navigation requirements.

5.2.5   GPS Altitude and Coordinates

GPS provides altitude information alongside coordinates. Understand the three-dimensional positioning with latitude, longitude, and altitude.

5.2.6   Accuracy in GPS Coordinates

GPS accuracy is influenced by factors like satellite geometry. The formula for GPS error is:

$$\text{GPS Error} = \text{User Range Error} + \text{Satellite Geometry Error}$$

Be aware of potential errors affecting the precision of GPS coordinates.

Understanding GPS coordinates is like deciphering a map to your destination. With latitude, longitude, and altitude, you navigate the world effortlessly.

5.3   Using GPS Devices

Master the art of GPS navigation devices effortlessly – a simplified approach without any mental pressure.

5.3.1   Powering On and Satellite Acquisition

$$\text{Time to First Fix (TTFF)} = \text{Time to Acquire Satellite Signals} + \text{Time for GPS Processing}$$

Understand the Time to First Fix (TTFF) by considering the time needed to acquire satellite signals and process GPS data.

5.3.2   Setting Waypoints

$$\text{Distance to Waypoint} = \sqrt{(\text{Latitude}_{\text{WP}} - \text{Latitude}_{\text{Current}})^2 + (\text{Longitude}_{\text{WP}} - \text{Longitude}_{\text{Current}})^2}$$

Calculate the distance to a waypoint using the GPS coordinates of the current location and the waypoint.

5.3.3   Navigating Routes

$$\text{Total Route Distance} = \sum_{i=1}^{n-1} \text{Distance Between Waypoints}_i$$

Determine the total distance of a route by summing the distances between consecutive waypoints.

5.3.4 Monitoring Speed and Pace

$$\text{Speed} = \frac{\text{Distance}}{\text{Time}}$$

Monitor your speed using GPS data by dividing the distance traveled by the time elapsed.

$$\text{Pace} = \frac{\text{Time}}{\text{Distance}}$$

Calculate your pace using GPS data by dividing the time elapsed by the distance traveled.

5.3.5 Elevation and Altitude Gain/Loss

$$\text{Altitude Gain/Loss} = \text{Final Altitude} - \text{Initial Altitude}$$

Determine the altitude gain or loss during a hike or journey using GPS altitude data.

5.3.6 Geocaching with GPS

$$\text{Geocaching Distance} = \sqrt{(\text{Latitude}_{\text{Cache}} - \text{Latitude}_{\text{Current}})^2 + (\text{Longitude}_{\text{Cache}} - \text{Longitude}_{\text{Current}})^2}$$

Calculate the distance to a geocache using the GPS coordinates of the current location and the cache.

5.3.7 Battery Conservation Tips

Extend GPS device battery life by adjusting settings, turning off unnecessary features, and carrying spare batteries.

Using GPS devices is like having a digital guide at your fingertips. Master these techniques, and your navigation becomes seamless and efficient.

5.4 Geocaching: A GPS Adventure

Embark on the thrilling GPS adventure of geocaching effortlessly – a simplified approach without any mental pressure.

### 5.4.1	Understanding Geocaching Coordinates

$$\text{Geocache Distance} = \sqrt{(\text{Latitude}_{\text{Cache}} - \text{Latitude}_{\text{Current}})^2 + (\text{Longitude}_{\text{Cache}} - \text{Longitude}_{\text{Current}})^2}$$

Calculate the distance to a geocache using the GPS coordinates of the current location and the cache.

### 5.4.2	Geocache Difficulty and Terrain Ratings

Geocaches have difficulty and terrain ratings. Difficulty ranges from 1 to 5, and terrain ranges from 1 to 5. A 1/1 geocache is considered easy to find and access, while a 5/5 is the most challenging.

### 5.4.3	Geocache Size and Types

Geocaches come in various sizes and types. Common sizes include micro, small, regular, and large. Types range from traditional caches to mystery caches and multi-caches.

### 5.4.4	Finding Geocaches with GPS Devices

$$\text{Total Geocache Distance} = \sum_{i=1}^{n} \text{Distance to Geocache}_i$$

Determine the total distance to multiple geocaches by summing the distances to each geocache.

### 5.4.5	Geocaching Tools and Equipment

Use tools like tweezers, penlights, and magnet extenders for efficient geocache retrieval. Carry spare logbooks and pencils.

### 5.4.6	Hiding Your Own Geocache

$$\text{Geocache Coordinates} = \text{Current Location Coordinates}$$

Set the coordinates of your geocache location to your current GPS coordinates for accurate placement.

### 5.4.7	Logging Geocache Finds

Log your geocache finds online. Include details like the difficulty faced, memorable moments, and any challenges encountered.

5.4.8 Respecting Nature and Local Regulations

Follow Leave No Trace principles and adhere to local geocaching guidelines and regulations. Respect nature and fellow geocachers.

Geocaching is like a treasure hunt powered by GPS. Let the coordinates guide you, and every find becomes an exciting adventure of exploration and discovery.

5.5 GPS Tips and Troubleshooting

Navigate smoothly and troubleshoot GPS issues effortlessly – a simplified approach without any mental pressure.

5.5.1 Maximizing Satellite Reception

$$\text{Satellite Elevation Angle} = \arcsin\left(\frac{\text{Satellite Altitude}}{\text{Distance to Satellite}}\right)$$

Maximize satellite reception by ensuring a clear line of sight. Calculate the satellite elevation angle for optimal positioning.

5.5.2 Calibrating Compass on GPS Devices

$$\text{Calibrated Compass Bearing} = \text{Magnetic Bearing} + \text{Magnetic Declination}$$

Calibrate the compass on your GPS device by adjusting the magnetic bearing with the magnetic declination for accurate readings.

5.5.3 Managing Battery Life

Extend GPS device battery life by adjusting screen brightness, using power-saving modes, and carrying spare batteries for longer journeys.

5.5.4 Using External Antennas

External antennas can enhance GPS signal reception. Connect external antennas for improved accuracy in challenging environments.

5.5.5   Dealing with GPS Drift

$$\text{GPS Drift Rate} = \frac{\text{Change in Position}}{\text{Time Interval}}$$

Handle GPS drift by calculating the drift rate. It indicates the change in position over a specific time interval.

5.5.6   Addressing GPS Accuracy Issues

$$\text{GPS Accuracy} = \text{User Range Error} + \text{Satellite Geometry Error}$$

Address GPS accuracy issues by understanding factors like user range error and satellite geometry error affecting precision.

5.5.7   Troubleshooting Signal Loss

Signal loss can occur due to obstacles or interference. Troubleshoot by adjusting your location or moving to an open area for better reception.

5.5.8   Data Management on GPS Devices

Manage GPS data efficiently by regularly updating maps, clearing unnecessary files, and organizing waypoints for smooth navigation.

GPS troubleshooting is like fine-tuning your navigation instrument. Master these tips, and your GPS becomes a reliable companion for all your adventures.

5.6   GPS vs. Traditional Navigation

Navigate effortlessly with GPS or embrace traditional methods – simplified for quick understanding.

5.6.1   Precision in Coordinates

GPS provides accurate coordinates:

$$\text{GPS Coordinates} = \text{Latitude} \pm \text{Longitude}$$

Traditional methods rely on maps and compasses for rough estimations.

5.6.2 Error Consideration

GPS has potential errors:

$$\text{GPS Error} = \text{User Range Error} + \text{Satellite Geometry Error}$$

Traditional navigation is less prone to such errors.

5.6.3 Quick Positioning

GPS offers quick positioning:

$$\text{Time to First Fix (TTFF)} = \text{Time to Acquire Satellite Signals} + \text{Time for GPS Processing}$$

Traditional methods may take longer for accurate positioning.

5.6.4 Terrain Adaptability

Traditional navigation excels in challenging terrains, using landmarks for effective route finding.

5.6.5 Battery Dependence

GPS relies on batteries, impacting navigation. Traditional tools like maps and compasses have no battery constraints.

5.6.6 Geocaching Adventure

Geocaching with GPS adds a high-tech, adventurous element:

$$\text{Geocache Distance} = \sqrt{(\text{Latitude}_{\text{Cache}} - \text{Latitude}_{\text{Current}})^2 + (\text{Longitude}_{\text{Cache}} - \text{Longitude}_{\text{Current}})^2}$$

Choose GPS for tech-driven adventures or embrace traditional methods for a classic approach. Mastering both offers a versatile navigation skill set.

Chapter 6

Map and Compass Integration

6.1 Combining Map and Compass Skills

Master the fusion of map and compass skills effortlessly – a simplified approach for seamless navigation.

6.1.1 Triangulation for Positioning

$$\text{Position} = \text{Intersection of Lines Drawn from Known Points on the Map}$$

Combine map and compass skills by triangulating your position using landmarks or features on the map.

6.1.2 Orienting the Map

$$\text{Oriented Map} = \text{Aligning Map's North to Compass North}$$

Integrate compass skills to orient the map, ensuring it aligns with the compass north for accurate navigation.

6.1.3 Measuring Distances

$$\text{Distance Measurement} = \text{Map's Scale} \times \text{Measured Distance on Map}$$

Use the compass to measure distances on the map by applying the map's scale factor.

6.1.4 Following Bearings

$$\text{Following a Bearing} = \text{Turning the Compass Dial to Match the Desired Bearing}$$

Navigate precisely by combining map readings and compass bearings. Align the compass dial with the desired bearing for accurate direction.

6.1.5 Adjusting for Declination

$$\text{Adjusted Bearing} = \text{Compass Bearing} + \text{Magnetic Declination}$$

Integrate declination adjustments when navigating with a compass to ensure true bearings align with the map.

6.1.6 Back Azimuth Calculation

$$\text{Back Azimuth} = \text{Compass Bearing} + 180°$$

Determine the opposite direction by calculating the back azimuth. Useful for retracing your steps or navigating back to a starting point.

6.1.7 Map and Compass Navigation Techniques

Blend map and compass techniques seamlessly for efficient navigation. Practice dead reckoning, terrain association, and pacing.

6.1.8 Emergency Navigation

$$\text{Emergency Direction} = \text{Known Location Direction} + \text{Estimated Distance}$$

In emergency situations, combine map and compass skills to navigate towards a known location by estimating the distance.

Map and compass integration is like having a powerful navigation duo. Master these skills, and you'll navigate through landscapes with confidence and precision.

6.2 Triangulation

Unlock the magic of triangulation effortlessly – a simplified approach for pinpoint accuracy in navigation.

6.2.1 Basic Triangulation Formula

Position = Intersection of Lines Drawn from Two Known Points on the Map

Master triangulation by drawing lines on the map from two visible landmarks to find your exact position.

6.2.2 Practical Triangulation Steps

1. **Identify Landmarks:** Spot two easily identifiable landmarks on the map and in your surroundings.
2. **Orient the Map:** Align the map with the actual landscape using a compass for accurate readings.
3. **Take Bearings:** Use the compass to measure the bearings (angles) from your location to each landmark.
4. **Plot Bearings on Map:** Draw lines on the map from each landmark in the direction of the measured bearings.
5. **Intersection Point:** The point where the lines intersect on the map is your precise location.

6.2.3 Advanced Triangulation Techniques

1. **Using More Landmarks:** Increase accuracy by taking bearings from three or more landmarks.
2. **Adjusting for Declination:** Correct compass readings by considering magnetic declination for precise triangulation.
3. **Back Bearings for Confirmation:** Take back bearings to confirm the accuracy of your initial triangulation.
4. **Distance Estimation:** Combine triangulation with distance estimation for even more accuracy in your position.

6.2.4 Emergency Triangulation

Emergency Direction = Known Landmark Direction + Estimated Distance

In emergency situations, use triangulation with a known landmark and estimated distance to navigate to safety.

Triangulation is your key to navigating with confidence. Master this technique, and you'll always find your way in the great outdoors.

6.3   Intersection Techniques

Master intersection techniques effortlessly – a simplified approach for quick and accurate navigation.

6.3.1   Position Fixing with Intersection

$$\text{Position} = \text{Intersection of Lines Drawn from Two Known Points on the Map}$$

Utilize intersection techniques by drawing lines from two known points on the map to pinpoint your exact location.

6.3.2   Landmarks as Reference Points

Choose prominent landmarks as reference points for intersection. Align the compass edge with the chosen landmarks for accurate lines.

6.3.3   Using Terrain Features

Identify distinctive terrain features such as peaks, valleys, or water bodies for intersection points. Use these features for precise navigation.

6.3.4   Practical Example

Imagine standing at point A and visually identifying two distinct landmarks (B and C) on the map. To find your position:

$$\text{Line AB} \cap \text{Line AC} = \text{Your Exact Position}$$

This simple intersection formula allows you to determine your position with ease.

6.3.5   Adjusting for Distance Estimation Errors

$$\text{Error Adjustment} = \text{Percentage Error} \times \text{Distance Traveled}$$

If you overestimate or underestimate distances, adjust your position by considering the percentage error in your estimation.

6.3.6 Multiple Intersection Points

$$\text{Position} = \text{Intersection of Lines from Multiple Known Points}$$

Enhance accuracy by using multiple known points on the map. Where lines intersect, you precisely determine your location.

6.3.7 Real-World Application

In the field, choose two or more visible points on the map, use the compass to draw lines, and locate yourself at the intersection. This practical approach ensures effective navigation.

6.3.8 Refining Skills through Practice

Intersection techniques improve with practice. Regularly challenge yourself to identify features, draw lines, and accurately locate your position.

Intersection techniques in map and compass integration provide a straightforward yet powerful method for finding your way in diverse landscapes.

6.4 Re-section Techniques

Master re-section techniques effortlessly – a simplified approach for quick and precise navigation.

6.4.1 Re-section Basics

Re-section involves determining your current location by identifying prominent features on the map.

6.4.2 Using Prominent Features

Identify at least two prominent features in the landscape that are also visible on the map.

6.4.3 Angle Measurement with Compass

$$\text{Angle to Feature} = \text{Compass Bearing to Feature} + \text{Magnetic Declination}$$

Measure the angle to each identified feature using the compass, adjusting for magnetic declination.

6.4.4   Drawing Lines on the Map

Draw lines on the map extending from each feature, following the measured angles.

6.4.5   Intersection Point

The point where the lines intersect on the map indicates your current location.

6.4.6   Error Considerations

$$\text{Error} = \text{Distance from Actual Position to Intersection Point}$$

Be aware of potential errors, considering the distance between your actual position and the intersection point.

6.4.7   Practical Tips

- Choose prominent features that are easily identifiable.

- Ensure accuracy in angle measurement with a properly calibrated compass.

- Double-check the intersection point for confidence in your re-section.

Re-section techniques provide a quick and effective method to pinpoint your location on the map, enhancing your navigation skills in the field.

6.5   Navigating without a Compass

Navigate without a compass effortlessly – a simplified approach using natural elements for orientation.

6.5.1   Solar Navigation

$$\text{Solar Time} = \text{Local Time} + \text{Equation of Time} + 4(\text{Standard Meridian} - \text{Local Meridian})$$

Use the sun's position to estimate directions. Solar time accounts for variations in the equation of time and local meridian.

6.5.2 Shadow-Tip Method

$$\text{Shadow Length} \propto \tan(\text{Sun's Elevation Angle})$$

Estimate directions by observing the length of shadows cast by objects. The shadow length is proportional to the tangent of the sun's elevation angle.

6.5.3 Natural Navigation Signs

- Moss tends to grow on the north side of trees in the Northern Hemisphere.
- Sun rises in the east and sets in the west.
- Stars like the North Star (Polaris) can guide you in the northern hemisphere.

6.5.4 Using Topography

$$\text{Water Flow Direction} \propto \text{Downhill Slope}$$

Observe the flow of water to determine downhill slopes. Water typically flows perpendicular to contour lines.

6.5.5 Time and Direction Relationship

$$15° \text{ of Earth's Rotation} \approx 1 \text{ Hour}$$

Use the Earth's rotation to estimate time based on the sun's position. Each 15 degrees of rotation corresponds to approximately 1 hour.

6.5.6 Celestial Navigation

Identify celestial bodies like the moon and planets for rough directional cues during nighttime navigation.

6.5.7 Practical Tips

- Be aware of your surroundings and the position of natural elements.
- Use multiple methods for increased accuracy.
- Practice navigating without a compass in familiar areas before relying on it in unknown terrains.
Navigating without a compass is a valuable skill that connects you with the environment, enhancing your ability to traverse landscapes confidently.

6.6   Advanced Map Reading Strategies

Master advanced map reading effortlessly – a simplified approach for precise navigation in diverse terrains.

6.6.1   Contour Line Interpretation

$$\text{Closer Contour Lines} = \text{Steep Terrain}$$

Read the contour lines to determine the steepness of the terrain. Closer contour lines indicate steeper slopes.

6.6.2   Understanding Map Colors

- Blue: Represents water bodies like rivers and lakes.
- Green: Indicates vegetation, forests, or grasslands.
- Brown: Represents contour lines and elevation changes.
- White: Depicts open areas or areas with less vegetation.

6.6.3   Map Gradient Interpretation

$$\text{Gradient} = \frac{\text{Change in Elevation}}{\text{Horizontal Distance}}$$

Calculate gradient using elevation changes and horizontal distance. Higher gradients indicate steeper slopes.

6.6.4   Map Datum and Coordinate Systems

Understand the map datum and coordinate system used in the map. Common datums include WGS 84 and NAD 27.

6.6.5   Advanced Map Symbols

Learn advanced symbols like geological formations, cultural features, and specific terrain indicators.

6.6.6   Using UTM Coordinates

$$\text{UTM Coordinates} = \text{Zone Number} + \text{Easting} + \text{Northing}$$

Utilize Universal Transverse Mercator (UTM) coordinates for precise positioning on the map.

6.6.7   Map Overlay Techniques

Overlay transparent sheets on the map for route planning, marking waypoints, or visualizing multiple map features.

6.6.8   Integrating GPS Data with Maps

$$\text{GPS Coordinates} = \text{Latitude} \pm \text{Longitude}$$

Combine GPS data seamlessly with map reading for accurate navigation and waypoint identification. Advanced map reading enhances your navigation skills, allowing you to interpret terrain features, use diverse map symbols, and integrate modern technologies for an optimal navigation experience.

Chapter 7

Navigating Waterways

7.1 Understanding Nautical Charts

Master nautical charts effortlessly – a simplified approach for smooth navigation on water.

7.1.1 Chart Basics

- **Scale:** Indicates the ratio of chart distance to actual distance.

- **Depth Soundings:** Represent water depths at specific locations.

- **Chart Datum:** The reference level for depth measurements.

- **Compass Rose:** Displays the variation between true and magnetic north.

7.1.2 Depth Measurement

$$\text{Depth Measurement} = \text{Charted Depth} - \text{Chart Datum}$$

Calculate the actual depth by subtracting the chart datum from the charted depth.

7.1.3 Tide Calculations

$$\text{Actual Depth} = \text{Charted Depth} + \text{Tide Height}$$

Adjust depth measurements for tide variations by adding the tide height to the charted depth.

7.1.4 Navigational Aids

- **Buoy Colors:** Red buoys are even-numbered and mark the starboard side of the channel. Green buoys are odd-numbered and mark the port side.

- **Lighthouses:** Serve as prominent day and night navigation markers.

7.1.5 Reading Loran Lines

$$\text{Loran Line} = \frac{\text{Difference in Time of Arrival (TOA)}}{\text{Loran Rate}}$$

Use Loran lines to navigate with electronic aids by calculating position based on time differences.

7.1.6 Understanding Tidal Currents

$$\text{Tidal Current Speed} = \text{Maximum Current Speed} \times \cos\left(\frac{\pi \times \text{Elapsed Time}}{\text{Tidal Cycle}}\right)$$

Estimate tidal current speed at any given time within the tidal cycle using elapsed time.

7.1.7 Practical Tips

- Memorize buoy color codes for quick identification.
- Keep chart datum adjustments in mind for accurate depth assessments.
- Be aware of tidal variations and their impact on water depth.

Understanding nautical charts ensures safe and confident navigation on water, utilizing key elements for precise and efficient waterway traversal.

7.2 Buoy Systems and Markers

Master buoy systems and markers effortlessly – a simplified approach for precise water navigation.

7.2.1 Buoy Color and Numbering

- **Red Buoys:** Even-numbered, mark the starboard side of the channel when entering from seaward.

- **Green Buoys:** Odd-numbered, mark the port side of the channel when entering from seaward.

- **Yellow Buoys:** Caution or warning buoys, often used for obstructions or special areas.

7.2.2 Lateral System

Safe Water Side = Side Opposite to the Main Channel

Identify the safe water side by choosing the side opposite to the main channel when navigating between red and green buoys.

7.2.3 Cardinal System

- **North Cardinal Buoy:** Points to safe water to the north.
- **East Cardinal Buoy:** Points to safe water to the east.
- **South Cardinal Buoy:** Points to safe water to the south.
- **West Cardinal Buoy:** Points to safe water to the west.

7.2.4 Isolated Danger and Special Purpose Buoys

- **Isolated Danger Buoy:** Indicates a specific danger with safe water surrounding it.
- **Special Purpose Buoy:** Marks areas like swimming zones, anchorages, or traffic separation schemes.

7.2.5 Light Characteristics

- **Flashing Light:** Periodic flashes.
- **Fixed Light:** Constant and non-flashing.
- **Occulting Light:** Regular periods of darkness between light.
- **Quick Flashing Light:** Faster periodic flashes.

7.2.6 Sound Signals

- **Single Short Blast:** I intend to pass you on my port side.
- **Single Long Blast:** I intend to pass you on my starboard side.
- **Two Short Blasts:** I am altering my course to starboard.

7.2.7 Practical Tips

- Memorize buoy color codes for quick identification. - Use cardinal buoys to determine the best direction to navigate around dangers.

- Recognize special purpose buoys for specific waterway information.

Understanding buoy systems and markers is crucial for safe and efficient water navigation, ensuring vessels navigate through channels and avoid potential hazards.

7.3   Tides and Currents

Master tides and currents effortlessly – a simplified approach for navigating waterways with ease.

7.3.1   Tidal Basics

- **High Tide:** Maximum water level.

- **Low Tide:** Minimum water level.

- **Flood Tide:** Incoming tide, rising water level.

- **Ebb Tide:** Outgoing tide, falling water level.

7.3.2   Tidal Range

$$\text{Tidal Range} = \text{High Tide} - \text{Low Tide}$$

Calculate the tidal range by subtracting the low tide from the high tide. A larger tidal range indicates more significant water level fluctuations.

7.3.3   Tidal Currents

- **Flood Current:** Inward flow of water during rising tide.

- **Ebb Current:** Outward flow of water during falling tide.

- **Slack Water:** Periods of minimal or no current flow between flood and ebb.

7.3.4   Rule of Twelfths

$$\text{Twelfths} = \frac{\text{Tidal Range}}{12}$$

Use the Rule of Twelfths to estimate tidal current strength at different intervals during the tidal cycle.

7.3.5   Navigating with Tides

- **High Tide:** Provides deeper water for navigation in shallow areas.

- **Low Tide:** Reveals potential obstacles and shallow spots.

- **Flood Tide:** Aids upstream navigation.

- **Ebb Tide:** Aids downstream navigation.

7.3.6   Coriolis Effect

- **Northern Hemisphere:** Tidal currents veer to the right.

- **Southern Hemisphere:** Tidal currents veer to the left.

7.3.7   Practical Tips

- Check tide tables for accurate high and low tide times.

- Be aware of tidal current strengths during navigation.

- Adjust navigation plans based on tidal conditions for safe and efficient water travel.

Understanding tides and currents is essential for safe navigation, ensuring vessels adapt to changing water levels and utilize tidal flow for efficient travel.

7.4   Navigation in Open Water

Master navigation in open water effortlessly – a simplified approach for smooth sailing and efficient travel.

7.4.1   Compass Navigation

$$\text{Steering Course} = \text{True Course} + \text{Deviation} + \text{Variation}$$

Use the compass for navigation by adjusting the true course for deviation and variation.

7.4.2   Dead Reckoning

$$\text{Estimated Position} = \text{Initial Position} + \text{Course Made Good} \times \text{Time}$$

Navigate by projecting your course and speed from the last known position, updating based on time and speed.

7.4.3   Piloting with Celestial Bodies

- **Sun:** Rises in the east, sets in the west.

- **Stars:** Use Polaris (North Star) for northern hemisphere navigation.

- **Moon:** Moonrise and moonset provide directional cues.

7.4.4   Electronic Navigation

- **GPS Coordinates:** Use latitude and longitude for precise positioning.

- **Chartplotter:** Display electronic charts with real-time vessel position.

7.4.5   Weather Observation

- **Wind Direction:** Observe wind patterns for sail or power adjustments.

- **Clouds:** High-altitude clouds may indicate approaching weather changes.

7.4.6   Wave Patterns

- **Wave Period:** Measure time between wave crests.
- **Wave Height:** Height from trough to crest.

7.4.7   Practical Tips

- Regularly check and update navigation instruments.
- Maintain a lookout for other vessels, especially in busy waterways.
- Keep a logbook for recording important navigation data.

Navigating in open water requires a combination of traditional and modern techniques. Be mindful of celestial cues, electronic aids, and environmental factors for a safe and enjoyable journey.

7.5   Safety Measures on Water

Master water safety effortlessly – a simplified approach for ensuring a secure and enjoyable water navigation experience.

7.5.1 Life Jackets

$$\text{Buoyancy Force} = \text{Weight of Water Displaced by Life Jacket}$$

Wear properly fitted life jackets for buoyancy, providing essential support in case of emergencies.

7.5.2 Navigation Lights

- **Red Port Light:** Indicates a vessel's port (left) side.
- **Green Starboard Light:** Indicates a vessel's starboard (right) side.
- **White Stern Light:** Indicates a vessel's stern (rear).

7.5.3 Sound Signals

- **One Short Blast:** I intend to pass you on my port side.
- **Two Short Blasts:** I intend to pass you on my starboard side.
- **Three Short Blasts:** I am operating in reverse.

7.5.4 Emergency Flares

Pyrotechnic Flares

Buoyant Smoke Signal

Handheld Flare

Use emergency flares to signal distress or your position during emergencies.

7.5.5 Man Overboard Procedures

- **Throw a Floatation Device:** Provide immediate buoyancy to the person in the water.
- **Alert Crew:** Use sound signals and alert the crew about the man overboard.
- **Circle the Person:** Safely maneuver the vessel to retrieve the person.

7.5.6 Weather Monitoring

- **Barometer:** Falling pressure indicates approaching bad weather.
- **Wind Shifts:** Sudden changes in wind direction may signal storms.

7.5.7   VHF Radio Communication

Mayday Call

Use VHF radio for distress calls. A Mayday call indicates a life-threatening emergency.

7.5.8   Practical Tips

- Conduct regular safety drills with the crew.
- Keep a first aid kit and emergency supplies on board.
- Stay updated on weather forecasts before setting sail.

Prioritize safety on the water by adhering to navigation rules, maintaining proper equipment, and being prepared for unexpected situations, ensuring a secure and enjoyable maritime experience.

7.6   River and Stream Navigation

Master river and stream navigation effortlessly – a simplified approach for safe and effective travel in flowing waters.

7.6.1   Understanding River Currents

$$\text{River Current Velocity} = \text{Average Speed} + \text{Eddies and Swirls}$$

Estimate river current velocity by considering the average speed and accounting for eddies and swirls.

7.6.2   Navigating Rapids

- **Eddy Lines:** Boundary between the main current and an eddy.
- **V-Wave Pattern:** Indicates rocks or obstacles beneath the water's surface.

7.6.3   Reading River Features

- **V-Shaped Ripples:** Shallow areas with potential obstacles.
- **Wider Sections:** Often signify deeper and slower-moving water.
- **Inside Bend Currents:** Slower currents compared to outside bends.

7.6.4 Avoiding Strainers

$$\text{Force on a Strainer} \propto \text{Current Velocity} \times \text{Strainer Surface Area}$$

Avoid strainers like overhanging branches, as the force exerted by the current increases with higher velocity and larger surface area.

7.6.5 River Crossing Techniques

- **Ferrying:** Move diagonally across the current to reach the opposite bank.
- **Angle Upstream:** Cross at an upstream angle to compensate for downstream drift.

7.6.6 Maneuvering with Oars or Paddles

- **Pivot Turn:** Use a paddle or oar as a pivot point for sharp turns.
- **Sweep Stroke:** Sweeping motion for wide turns.
- **Draw Stroke:** Pull the paddle or oar towards the boat for lateral movement.

7.6.7 Practical Tips

- Scout the river before navigating unfamiliar stretches.
- Communicate effectively with your crew during maneuvers.
- Wear appropriate safety gear, including helmets in rough water.

Navigating rivers and streams requires a combination of understanding currents, reading water features, and employing effective paddling techniques. Stay attentive to the water's behavior for a safe and enjoyable journey.

7.7 Coastal Navigation

Master coastal navigation effortlessly – a simplified approach for smooth sailing along coastlines.

7.7.1 Navigational Aids

- **Lighthouses:** Prominent markers for identifying coastal features.
- **Beacons:** Mark specific points or dangers along the coast.
- **Daymarks:** Visual aids, often painted or shaped for easy recognition.

7.7.2   Understanding Coastal Currents

$$\text{Coastal Current Speed} = \text{Wind Speed} + \text{Tidal Current}$$

Estimate coastal current speed by combining the wind speed with tidal currents.

7.7.3   Beach Characteristics

- **Longshore Drift:** Movement of water along the shoreline.
- **Sandbars:** Submerged or partially exposed bars of sand.

7.7.4   Tidal Fluctuations

- **High Tide:** Expands navigable areas.
- **Low Tide:** Reveals potential hazards and shallow spots.

7.7.5   Navigation in Fog

- **Fog Signal:** Use sound signals at regular intervals.
- **Radar Navigation:** Rely on radar for positioning in low visibility.

7.7.6   Rock and Reef Navigation

$$\text{Time to Collision} = \frac{\text{Distance to Object}}{\text{Speed Over Ground}}$$

Calculate time to collision by dividing the distance to an object by the vessel's speed over ground.

7.7.7   Maneuvering in Shallow Waters

- **Reduce Speed:** Decrease speed to minimize the risk of grounding.
- **Use Depth Sounder:** Monitor water depth for safe navigation.

7.7.8   Practical Tips

- Stay alert to changes in coastal features and water conditions.
- Regularly check navigational aids for accurate position reference.
- Utilize electronic charts and GPS for precise coastal navigation.

Coastal navigation demands awareness of navigational aids, understanding tidal patterns, and adapting to changing conditions. Safely sail along coastlines by combining traditional and modern techniques for a seamless maritime experience.

Chapter 8

Advanced Mapping Technologies

8.1 GIS (Geographic Information System)

Unlock the power of GIS effortlessly – a simplified approach for harnessing geographic information for advanced mapping.

8.1.1 GIS Components

- **Spatial Data:** Information with a geographic or spatial component.
- **Attribute Data:** Non-spatial information linked to spatial data.
- **Software:** Applications for analyzing and visualizing geographic data.

8.1.2 Coordinate Systems

- **Latitude and Longitude:** Global coordinate system based on Earth's equator and meridians.
- **UTM (Universal Transverse Mercator):** Divides the world into zones for localized mapping.

8.1.3 GIS Mapping Functions

Buffer Analysis

Create buffers around specific geographic features to analyze and visualize the surrounding area.

Overlay Analysis

Combine multiple layers of spatial data to identify intersections and relationships.

Spatial Query

Retrieve specific geographic information based on user-defined criteria.

8.1.4 Remote Sensing Integration

- **Satellite Imagery:** Capture high-resolution images of Earth's surface.

- **Aerial Photography:** Obtain detailed views from aircraft.

8.1.5 Topological Relationships

- **Adjacent:** Spatial features sharing a common boundary.

- **Connected:** Features linked by a shared point or line.

8.1.6 3D Mapping

3D Visualization

Use GIS to create three-dimensional representations of geographic features for enhanced visualization.

8.1.7 Practical Tips

- Understand the coordinate system used in GIS data.

- Learn to interpret spatial relationships for effective analysis.

- Explore GIS software capabilities for specific mapping needs.

GIS transforms how we analyze and visualize geographic data, offering powerful tools for decision-making and comprehensive mapping. Embrace the potential of GIS for advanced mapping applications effortlessly.

8.2 Remote Sensing

Tap into the potential of remote sensing effortlessly – a simplified approach for collecting information about Earth's surface from a distance.

8.2.1 Satellite Remote Sensing

- **Passive Sensors:** Measure natural energy (sunlight) reflected or emitted by Earth. - **Active Sensors:** Transmit energy and measure the return signal.

8.2.2 Electromagnetic Spectrum

- **Visible Light:** Detected by the human eye, used in optical imagery.
- **Infrared:** Useful for vegetation health analysis.
- **Microwave:** Penetrates clouds and can be used for all-weather imaging.

8.2.3 Resolution in Remote Sensing

$$\text{Spatial Resolution} \times \text{Spectral Resolution} \times \text{Temporal Resolution}$$

Combine spatial, spectral, and temporal resolutions for comprehensive remote sensing capabilities.

8.2.4 Image Interpretation

- **Pixel Analysis:** Examine individual image elements.
- **Feature Recognition:** Identify distinct features within an image.
- **Change Detection:** Monitor changes in Earth's surface over time.

8.2.5 Orthorectification

$$\text{Orthorectified Image} = \text{Raw Image} + \text{Terrain Correction}$$

Correct images for terrain distortion, ensuring accurate spatial representation.

8.2.6 Applications of Remote Sensing

- **Land Use Planning:** Monitor urban development and agricultural patterns.
- **Environmental Monitoring:** Track deforestation, climate change, and habitat loss.
- **Disaster Management:** Assess and respond to natural disasters.

8.2.7 Practical Tips

- Understand the characteristics of different remote sensing platforms.

- Familiarize yourself with image processing techniques.

- Stay updated on advancements in remote sensing technology.

Remote sensing revolutionizes our understanding of Earth's surface. Utilize its capabilities for informed decision-making, environmental monitoring, and comprehensive mapping with ease.

8.3 Augmented Reality in Navigation

Dive into the world of augmented reality effortlessly – a simplified approach for enhancing navigation through real-time digital overlays.

8.3.1 Components of Augmented Reality (AR)

- **Real-world View:** The physical environment observed through a device.

- **Digital Overlay:** Computer-generated information superimposed on the real-world view.

8.3.2 AR in Navigation

- **Head-Up Displays (HUD):** Project navigational information onto the windshield.

- **Smartphone Apps:** Overlay directions and points of interest on the live camera feed.

8.3.3 AR Navigation Algorithms

$$\text{AR Navigation Accuracy} = \frac{\text{Device Position Accuracy} + \text{Sensor Accuracy}}{\text{Number of Sensors}}$$

Improve AR navigation accuracy by considering the accuracy of the device's position and sensors.

8.3.4 Wayfinding with AR

- **Turn-by-Turn Directions:** Visual cues overlaid on the real-world view.

- **Destination Markers:** Digital markers guiding towards the destination.

- **Points of Interest:** Information about nearby landmarks and attractions.

8.3.5 Interactive Mapping

- **Gesture Control:** Navigate through maps using hand gestures.

- **Voice Commands:** Interact with AR navigation using voice inputs.

8.3.6 AR for Outdoor Exploration

- **Hiking Trails:** Overlay trail information on a natural landscape.

- **Tourist Attractions:** Augmented information about historical sites.

8.3.7 Practical Tips

- Ensure a clear line of sight for optimal AR functionality. - Regularly update AR apps for the latest mapping data. - Familiarize yourself with AR gestures and voice commands.

Augmented reality transforms navigation by blending digital information seamlessly with the real world. Embrace AR for an interactive and immersive navigation experience with ease.

8.4 Mapping Apps and Software

Embark on a journey through mapping apps and software effortlessly – a simplified guide to enhance your mapping experience.

8.4.1 Key Features of Mapping Apps

- **Real-Time Navigation:** Receive turn-by-turn directions for optimal routes.

- **Traffic Updates:** Stay informed about current road conditions and congestion.

- **Offline Maps:** Download maps for use in areas with limited or no connectivity.

8.4.2 Popular Mapping Apps

1. **Google Maps:**

- **Features:** Street view, live traffic updates, and business information.

- **Navigation Tips:** Utilize voice commands for hands-free guidance.

2. **Waze:**

- **Features:** Community-driven traffic data, real-time alerts, and shortcuts.

- **Navigation Tips:** Collaborate with other users to share real-time information.

3. **Apple Maps:**

- **Features:** Integration with Apple ecosystem, indoor maps, and Flyover mode.

- **Navigation Tips:** Use the 'Look Around' feature for immersive street-level views.

8.4.3   GIS Software for Professionals

1. **ArcGIS:**

- **Features:** Comprehensive mapping and spatial analysis tools.

- **Applications:** Urban planning, environmental monitoring, and more.

2. **QGIS:**

- **Features:** Open-source GIS software with a user-friendly interface.

- **Applications:** Cartography, data analysis, and visualization.

8.4.4   Integration with GPS Technology

- **GPS Tracking:** Utilize GPS signals for accurate location tracking.

- **Geotagging:** Embed geographic coordinates in photos or data points.

8.4.5   Augmented Reality Integration

- **AR Navigation Overlays:** Enhance navigation with real-time digital information.

- **Digital Mapping Layers:** Superimpose digital data on the real-world view.

8.4.6   Practical Tips

- Explore the features of different mapping apps to find the one that suits your needs. - Stay updated on software enhancements and new features. - Familiarize yourself with the integration of mapping apps with other technologies.

Mapping apps and software simplify navigation, offer real-time information, and empower professionals with advanced GIS tools. Navigate confidently and explore the world with the aid of cutting-edge mapping technologies effortlessly.

8.5　Emerging Technologies in Map Reading

Embark on the future of map reading effortlessly – a simplified guide to emerging technologies shaping the way we navigate and understand our surroundings.

8.5.1　LiDAR Technology

- **Principle:** Measures distances using laser light to create detailed, three-dimensional maps.
- **Applications:** Autonomous vehicles, forestry, and environmental modeling.

8.5.2　Drone Mapping

- **Advantages:** Aerial perspective for high-resolution mapping and surveying.
- **Applications:** Agriculture, construction site monitoring, and disaster assessment.

8.5.3　Blockchain in Mapping

- **Benefits:** Secure and transparent storage of mapping data.
- **Applications:** Land registry, property transactions, and decentralized mapping platforms.

8.5.4　5G Technology

- **Enhancements:** Faster data transfer and reduced latency.
- **Applications:** Real-time mapping updates, augmented reality navigation.

8.5.5　Artificial Intelligence (AI) in Map Analysis

- **Capabilities:** Automated interpretation of satellite imagery and map data.
- **Applications:** Land cover classification, object detection, and anomaly identification.

8.5.6　Quantum Mapping

- **Potential:** Quantum computing for complex mapping algorithms.
- **Applications:** Optimization problems, large-scale spatial analysis.

8.5.7   Spatial Augmented Reality (SAR)

- **Advancements:** Real-time projection of digital information onto physical objects.
- **Applications:** Enhanced navigation, interactive spatial visualization.

8.5.8   Practical Tips

- Stay informed about the latest developments in mapping technologies.
- Explore the practical applications of emerging technologies in your field.
- Consider the integration of multiple technologies for comprehensive map analysis.

Emerging technologies are revolutionizing map reading, offering innovative solutions for a wide range of industries. Embrace these advancements to navigate and analyze spatial data effortlessly.

8.6   Future Trends in Map Navigation

Embark on a journey into the future of map navigation effortlessly – a simplified guide to the upcoming trends shaping the way we explore and understand our world.

8.6.1   Artificial Intelligence (AI) Integration

- **Predictive Analytics:** AI algorithms predicting optimal routes based on historical data.
- **Personalized Recommendations:** AI-driven suggestions for points of interest and destinations.

8.6.2   Integration of Virtual Reality (VR)

- **Immersive Exploration:** Virtual tours and simulations for in-depth map exploration.
- **VR-enhanced Wayfinding:** Navigating through virtual representations of physical spaces.

8.6.3   Blockchain for Decentralized Mapping

- **Data Ownership:** Users have control over their mapping data through blockchain.
- **Decentralized Mapping Platforms:** Community-driven and secure map creation and updates.

8.6.4   Advancements in Holographic Displays

- **Holographic Maps:** Three-dimensional, interactive holographic representations of maps.
- **Spatial Interaction:** Users can manipulate and interact with holographic map elements.

8.6.5   Biometric Integration for Navigation

- **Gesture-based Commands:** Navigate maps using hand gestures and biometric inputs.

- **Eye-tracking Technology:** Control map movement and features through eye movements.

8.6.6   Smart Infrastructure Integration

- **Connected Cities:** Integration of maps with smart city infrastructure for real-time updates.
- **Internet of Things (IoT) Integration:** Mapping data from various IoT devices for comprehensive analysis.

8.6.7   Environmental Mapping for Sustainability

- **Climate Impact Maps:** Visualizing the environmental impact of human activities.
- **Sustainable Navigation Routes:** Recommending eco-friendly travel options.

8.6.8   Practical Tips

- Stay curious and open to adopting new technologies in map navigation.
- Experiment with emerging trends in controlled environments to understand their practicality.
- Collaborate with communities and organizations driving innovations in map navigation.

The future of map navigation holds exciting possibilities, incorporating advanced technologies for more intuitive, immersive, and sustainable exploration of our surroundings.

Chapter 9

Emergency Navigation Skills

9.1 Lost in the Wilderness: What to Do

Navigate the wilderness with ease even when lost – a simplified guide to practical actions and strategies for survival.

9.1.1 STOP Method

- **Stop:** Pause and take a moment to assess your surroundings.

- **Think:** Evaluate your situation, available resources, and potential hazards.

- **Observe:** Look for landmarks, listen for sounds, and note any signs of civilization.

- **Plan:** Develop a simple plan based on your observations for the next steps.

9.1.2 Navigational Tools

- **Compass and Map:** Orient yourself using a map and compass if available.

- **Sun and Shadows:** Determine cardinal directions by observing the sun and shadows.

9.1.3 Building a Shelter

- **Natural Shelters:** Look for caves, overhangs, or thick foliage for protection.

- **Emergency Shelter:** Construct a simple shelter using available materials.

9.1.4 Water Sourcing

- **Streams and Rivers:** Follow downhill to find water sources.
- **Rainwater Collection:** Use clothing or a container to collect rainwater.

9.1.5 Fire Building

- **Fire for Warmth:** Create a fire for warmth during cold nights.
- **Signal Fire:** Use a well-constructed fire as a distress signal.

9.1.6 Food Gathering

- **Edible Plants:** Identify safe, edible plants if knowledgeable.
- **Insects and Small Animals:** Use simple traps or gather insects for sustenance.

9.1.7 Signaling for Help

- **Auditory Signals:** Yell, use a whistle, or create loud sounds to attract attention.
- **Visual Signals:** Use reflective materials, bright clothing, or create visible symbols.

9.1.8 Practical Tips

- Stay calm and focused to make rational decisions. - Prioritize basic survival needs: shelter, water, fire, and food. - Preserve energy by avoiding unnecessary movements.

Navigating the wilderness when lost becomes manageable with practical strategies and essential survival skills. Stay composed, assess your surroundings, and take deliberate steps towards safety and rescue.

9.2 Emergency Shelter Building

Master the art of building emergency shelters effortlessly – a simplified guide to creating temporary shelters for survival.

9.2.1 Shelter Types

1. **Lean-to Shelter:**

- **Materials:** Long branches, logs, and a tarp or large leaves.

- **Construction:** Lean one side against a sturdy object, forming an A-frame.

2. **Debris Hut:**

- **Materials:** Branches, leaves, and any available debris.

- **Construction:** Create a frame with branches and cover it with leaves and debris.

3. **Tarp Shelter:**

- **Materials:** Tarp or any waterproof material and paracord or vines.

- **Construction:** Secure the tarp overhead using a ridgeline and stakes.

4. **Snow Cave:**

- **Materials:** Packed snow or ice.

- **Construction:** Dig into a snowbank, creating an insulated space.

5. **A-frame Shelter:** - **Materials:** Long branches or poles, and a tarp or large leaves.

- **Construction:** Form an A-frame using the branches and cover with the tarp.

9.2.2   Shelter Building Tips

- **Location:** Choose a flat, elevated area away from potential hazards.

- **Insulation:** Use natural materials for bedding and insulation from the ground.

- **Ventilation:** Ensure proper airflow to prevent condensation inside the shelter.

- **Visibility:** Make your shelter visible for rescue teams using bright colors or reflective materials.

9.2.3   Emergency Sleeping Bag

- **Materials:** Emergency or space blanket.

- **Usage:** Wrap yourself in the blanket for added warmth and insulation.

9.2.4   Practical Tips

- Practice building shelters in a controlled environment.

- Utilize available materials efficiently to save energy.

- Prioritize quick and effective shelter construction.

Mastering emergency shelter building skills ensures you can create a safe and protective space in challenging situations. Whether in the wilderness or unexpected circumstances, these practical techniques will aid in your survival.

9.3   Using Natural Indicators for Direction

Navigate with nature effortlessly – a simplified guide to using natural cues for finding direction in emergency situations.

9.3.1   Sun as a Compass

- **Morning Sun:** Faces east during sunrise.

- **Midday Sun:** Faces south at its highest point.

- **Evening Sun:** Sets in the west.

9.3.2   Shadow Stick Method

1. **Place a Stick Upright:** Position a straight stick vertically in the ground.

2. **Mark the Tip of the Shadow:** Mark the tip of the shadow with a small stone.

3. **Wait for 15 Minutes:** After 15 minutes, mark the new tip of the shadow.

4. **Line Connecting Marks:** Draw a line connecting the two marks.

5. **East-West Direction:** The line points east-west, with the first mark indicating west.

9.3.3   North Star (Polaris)

- **Locate the Big Dipper:** Find the Big Dipper constellation.

- **Draw an Imaginary Line:** Draw an imaginary line from the two outer stars of the Big Dipper.

- **Find the North Star:** The line points towards the North Star.

9.3.4   Moon Phases

- **Waxing Crescent:** Points towards the west.

- **Waning Crescent:** Points towards the east.

9.3.5   Navigating by Plants

- **Moss on Trees:** Typically grows on the north side of trees.

- **Sunflower Heads:** Face east in the morning and west in the afternoon.

9.3.6   Practical Tips

- Observe your surroundings and identify natural indicators.

- Use multiple methods for confirmation and accuracy.

- Practice these techniques in different environments for familiarity.

Master the art of using natural indicators for direction, making navigation in emergency situations intuitive and straightforward. Trust in the wisdom of nature to guide you safely.

9.4   Signal Techniques

Master the art of signaling effortlessly – a simplified guide to attracting attention and calling for help in emergency situations.

9.4.1   Auditory Signals

1. **Whistle Blast:**

- **Pattern:** Three short blasts.

- **Meaning:** International distress signal; indicates you need help.

2. **Yelling or Shouting:**

- **Pattern:** Repeated shouts.

- **Meaning:** Call out "Help!" or use other loud noises to alert nearby individuals.

3. **Drumming or Beating:**

- **Pattern:** Consistent beats.

- **Meaning:** Creates a rhythmic sound that can travel over long distances.

9.4.2   Visual Signals

1. **Reflective Materials:**

- **Using Sunlight:** Reflect sunlight with a mirror or any reflective object.

- **Using Flashlight:** Signal with flashlight beams in a repetitive pattern.

2. **Bright Clothing or Objects:**

- **Create Contrast:** Wear or display bright colors for visibility against natural surroundings.

3. **Signal Fire:**

- **Build a Fire:** Use green vegetation to produce smoke for increased visibility.

- **Flashing Flames:** Create flashes by blocking and unblocking the fire source.

9.4.3   Ground Signals

1. **SOS Symbol:**

- **Digging or Arranging Objects:** Form the international SOS signal in open areas.

2. **Large Arrows:**

- **Use Rocks or Logs:** Create arrows pointing towards your location.

3. **Use of Color Contrast:**

- **Bright Against Dark:** Arrange items in a way that creates color contrast for aerial visibility.

9.4.4   Practical Tips

- Choose signaling methods based on the situation and available resources.
- Consistency in signals helps distinguish them from natural occurrences.
- Signal during daylight hours for maximum visibility.

Master these practical signaling techniques to increase your chances of rescue and ensure effective communication in emergency scenarios. Stay visible and audible to those who can provide assistance.

9.5   Navigation in Extreme Conditions

Navigate through the harshest conditions with ease – a simplified guide to survival navigation in extreme environments.

9.5.1   Snow and Ice Navigation

1. **Snow Depth Estimation:**

- **Using Stick or Pole:** Insert a stick vertically to estimate snow depth.
- **Knee Rule:** Measure snow depth by comparing it to your knee.

2. **Identifying Snowdrifts:**

- **Look for Shapes:** Recognize patterns indicating wind-formed snowdrifts.
- **Windward Side:** Drifts usually form on the windward side of obstacles.

3. **Using Shadows for Direction:**

- **Shadow Stick Method:** Determine cardinal directions with shadows.

- **North-Facing Slopes:** Tend to have more snow and ice.

9.5.2 Desert Navigation

1. **Reading Sand Dunes:**

- **Crescent Shape:** Dunes generally have a crescent shape due to prevailing winds.

- **Windward and Leeward Sides:** Slope on the windward side is gentle, while the leeward side is steeper.

2. **Navigating by Stars:**

- **Clear Night Sky:** Stars can provide orientation in the absence of landmarks.

- **Polaris for Direction:** Locate Polaris for north reference.

3. **Conserving Water:**

- **Morning Dew:** Collect dew from plants or structures in the morning.

- **Urination Frequency:** Monitor hydration levels by urine color and frequency.

9.5.3 Jungle and Rainforest Navigation

1. **Navigating Waterways:**

- **Following Streams:** Streams often lead to larger water sources.

- **Animal Trails:** Follow animal trails, as they may lead to water.

2. **Identifying Edible Plants:**

- **Local Knowledge:** Learn about local flora from indigenous communities.

- **Universal Edibility Test:** Test plants for edibility in uncertain areas.

3. **Utilizing Sun Patterns:**

- **Breaks in Canopy:** Observe sun patterns through breaks in the jungle canopy.

- **Directional Growth:** Plants often grow towards sunlight.

9.5.4 Extreme Temperature Survival

1. **Layering Clothing:**

- **Base Layer:** Moisture-wicking material to keep skin dry.

- **Insulation Layer:** Retain body heat with insulating materials.

- **Outer Shell:** Protect from wind, rain, or snow.

2. **Hydration Management:**

- **Monitoring Sweat Loss:** Adjust water intake based on sweating.

- **Electrolyte Replacement:** Consume electrolyte-rich fluids.

3. **Shelter Construction:**

- **Reflective Materials:** Use reflective materials to bounce off or trap heat.

- **Body Heat Preservation:** Build small shelters to conserve body heat.

9.5.5 Practical Tips

- Adapt navigation techniques based on the specific conditions.

- Prioritize safety and conserving energy in extreme environments.

- Stay calm and focused on the immediate survival needs.

Master the skills for navigating in extreme conditions, ensuring your ability to find your way and survive even in the toughest environments. Be prepared, stay vigilant, and conquer the challenges presented by extreme circumstances.

9.6 Survival Navigation Strategies

Master the essentials of survival navigation – a simplified guide to finding your way and staying alive in challenging situations.

9.6.1 Stay Calm and Assess

1. **Pause and Observe:**

- **Assess the Situation:** Take a moment to understand your surroundings.

- **Identify Landmarks:** Look for any recognizable features.

2. **Control Panic:**

- **Deep Breathing:** Inhale and exhale slowly to calm nerves.

- **Focus on Solutions:** Shift focus from panic to finding solutions.

9.6.2 Prioritize Basic Needs

1. **Water Sources:**

- **Natural Indicators:** Look for signs of water such as vegetation or animal activity.

- **Collect Rainwater:** Use containers or clothing to catch rain.

2. **Shelter Construction:**

- **Utilize Natural Resources:** Build shelters using available materials.

- **Preserve Body Heat:** Create small, insulated spaces for warmth.

9.6.3   Navigation Techniques

1. **Solar Navigation:**

- **Shadow Stick Method:** Use a stick to track the movement of the sun.

- **Sunrise and Sunset:** Determine east and west for direction.

2. **Star Navigation:**

- **North Star (Polaris):** Locate Polaris for north reference.

- **Constellation Recognition:** Identify prominent constellations.

3. **Improvised Compass:**

- **Magnetic Needle:** Rub a needle against clothing to magnetize it.

- **Floatation Method:** Place the needle on a leaf in water, aligning it with the north.

9.6.4   Signaling for Rescue

1. **Auditory Signals:**

- **Whistle Blasts:** Use three short blasts as an international distress signal.

- **Yelling or Shouting:** Call for help loudly and repeatedly.

2. **Visual Signals:**

- **Reflective Materials:** Use mirrors or bright objects to reflect sunlight.

- **Signal Fires:** Build fires using green vegetation for smoke.

9.6.5   Practical Tips

- Adapt strategies based on the environment and available resources. - Conserve energy and stay hydrated to maintain physical and mental strength. - Signal consistently and use a combination of methods for better visibility.

Navigate through survival scenarios with confidence, utilizing practical and effective strategies to ensure your safety and well-being. Stay focused, stay resourceful, and increase your chances of rescue with these essential survival navigation techniques.

Chapter 10

Cultural and Historical Maps

10.1 Historical Maps: A Window to the Past

Unlock the secrets of the past with historical maps – a quick and captivating exploration into the world of historical cartography.

10.1.1 Understanding Historical Maps

1. **Map Evolution:**
- **Timeline Depiction:** Historical maps showcase changes in borders, cities, and territories over time.
- **Evolution of Cartography:** Witness advancements in mapmaking techniques and styles.
2. **Interpreting Symbols:**
- **Political Boundaries:** Dotted lines, colors, or symbols denote political divisions.
- **Trade Routes:** Arrows or pathways illustrate historical trade routes.

10.1.2 Key Features of Historical Maps

1. **Battlefield Maps:**
- **Tactical Insights:** Understand the strategies and movements of armies.
- **Topography Representation:** Hills, rivers, and forests impact battle outcomes.
2. **Exploration and Discovery:**
- **Uncharted Territories:** Explore regions yet to be fully explored or documented.

- **Sea Voyages:** Trace the routes of famous explorers and navigators.

3. **Cultural Maps:**

- **Distribution of Cultures:** Visualize the spread and influence of civilizations.

- **Language and Religion:** Maps reflect linguistic and religious diversity.

10.1.3   Practical Insights from Historical Maps

1. **Urban Development:**

- **City Expansion:** Observe the growth and development of urban areas.

- **Architectural Changes:** Identify historical landmarks and structures.

2. **Transportation Networks:**

- **Historical Trade Routes:** Map the movement of goods and commodities.

- **Development of Railways:** Witness the impact of railways on transportation.

3. **Environmental Changes:**

- **Land Use Patterns:** Track changes in agriculture and deforestation.

- **Natural Disasters:** Explore maps reflecting the aftermath of earthquakes, floods, and other events.

10.1.4   Preservation and Accessibility

1. **Digital Archives:**

- **Online Repositories:** Access historical maps through digital platforms.

- **Georeferencing Techniques:** Enhance accuracy and overlay historical maps on modern ones.

2. **Historical GIS:**

- **Spatial Analysis:** Use Geographic Information Systems to analyze historical data.

- **Overlaying Layers:** Compare historical maps with current landscapes for insights.

10.1.5   Practical Tips

- Explore historical maps interactively to enhance learning and understanding.

- Utilize digital tools to overlay historical maps on contemporary ones for comparative analysis.

- Connect with historical societies and archives for access to rare and unique maps.

Embark on a visual journey through time with historical maps, gaining a unique perspective on the cultural, political, and geographical changes that have shaped our world. Dive into the richness of history and witness the evolution of landscapes and civilizations through the lens of historical cartography.

10.2 Cultural Mapping

Embark on a journey through cultures with a simplified guide to cultural mapping – unlocking the richness and diversity of communities around the world.

10.2.1 Understanding Cultural Mapping

1. **Definition:**
- **Cultural Mapping:** A method to visually represent and understand the cultural aspects of a community or region.
2. **Elements of Cultural Mapping:**
- **Cultural Practices:** Identify rituals, traditions, and ceremonies.
- **Cultural Spaces:** Highlight locations significant to a community.
- **Cultural Artifacts:** Represent symbols, art, and historical artifacts.

10.2.2 Practical Steps in Cultural Mapping

1. **Community Engagement:**
- **Community Participation:** Involve locals in sharing their cultural insights.
- **Interviews and Surveys:** Conduct interviews to gather personal narratives.
2. **Mapping Cultural Practices:**
- **Symbolic Representation:** Use symbols or icons to represent cultural practices.
- **Timeline Mapping:** Create a timeline showcasing the evolution of cultural practices.
3. **Identifying Cultural Spaces:**
- **Landmarks and Monuments:** Mark significant landmarks with cultural importance.
- **Sacred Sites:** Identify places with spiritual or religious significance.

10.2.3 Benefits of Cultural Mapping

1. **Preservation of Culture:**
- **Documentation:** Preserve cultural heritage through visual representation.

- **Knowledge Transfer:** Facilitate the transfer of cultural knowledge across generations.

2. **Community Empowerment:**

- **Community-Led Development:** Foster community-led initiatives and development.

- **Resource Allocation:** Aid in resource allocation for cultural preservation.

3. **Tourism and Cultural Exchange:**

- **Cultural Tourism:** Attract tourists interested in cultural experiences.

- **Global Collaboration:** Facilitate cultural exchange and collaboration.

10.2.4   Challenges and Considerations

1. **Ethical Considerations:**

- **Informed Consent:** Obtain informed consent when documenting cultural practices.

- **Respect for Privacy:** Balance documentation with respect for cultural privacy.

2. **Dynamic Nature of Culture:**

- **Adaptability:** Recognize that cultures evolve and adapt over time.

- **Ongoing Mapping:** Continuously update cultural maps to reflect changes.

10.2.5   Practical Tips

- Utilize symbols, colors, and annotations to enhance the visual appeal of cultural maps. - Foster collaboration between mapmakers and local communities for accurate representation. - Emphasize the importance of cultural sensitivity and ethical practices in cultural mapping.

Embark on a cultural journey through the art of mapping, exploring the vibrant tapestry of traditions, practices, and spaces that define the essence of diverse communities.

10.3   Reading Heritage Maps

Explore the rich tapestry of history through heritage maps – a quick and accessible guide to decoding cultural and historical information.

10.3.1   Interpreting Symbols and Icons

1. **Monuments and Landmarks:**

- **Symbol Recognition:** Learn symbols representing historical sites and landmarks.

- **Iconography Understanding:** Decode statues, memorials, and architectural symbols.

2. **Historical Routes:**

- **Trail Markings:** Understand symbols denoting historical routes and journeys.

- **Pilgrimage Paths:** Identify paths of cultural or religious significance.

10.3.2   Understanding Chronology

1. **Time Scales:**

- **Eras and Periods:** Recognize visual cues representing different historical eras.

- **Timeline Integration:** Maps may incorporate timelines for chronological understanding.

2. **Evolution of Settlements:**

- **Urban Growth Patterns:** Track the development of cities and towns over time.

- **Expansion and Contraction:** Understand historical changes in borders and territories.

10.3.3   Cultural and Ethnic Mapping

1. **Population Distribution:**

- **Density Indicators:** Visualize the concentration of different communities.

- **Migration Patterns:** Explore historical movements of ethnic groups.

2. **Cultural Heritage Zones:**

- **World Heritage Sites:** Identify locations recognized for their cultural significance.

- **Intangible Cultural Heritage:** Understand areas with rich intangible cultural practices.

10.3.4   Technological Advancements

1. **Overlaying Historical Maps:**

- **GIS Integration:** Use Geographic Information Systems for layered historical maps.

- **Satellite Imagery Comparison:** Compare modern satellite imagery with historical maps.

2. **Digital Reconstructions:**

- **Virtual Heritage Tours:** Experience historical sites through digital reconstructions.

- **Augmented Reality Applications:** Overlay historical information on real-world views.

10.3.5 Practical Tips

- Familiarize yourself with the key symbols and conventions used on heritage maps. - Cross-reference historical maps with contemporary sources for comprehensive understanding. - Embrace technology for immersive experiences in exploring cultural and historical landscapes.

Unlock the stories embedded in heritage maps, gaining insights into the cultural and historical evolution of regions. Decode the past effortlessly, connecting with the cultural tapestry of our ancestors through the language of maps.

10.4 Tourist and Heritage Navigation

Embark on a journey through time and culture with tourist and heritage navigation – a swift guide to navigating historical sites and cultural landmarks with ease.

10.4.1 Planning Your Heritage Tour

1. **Site Selection:**

- **Researching Destinations:** Utilize travel guides and online resources.

- **Cultural Interest:** Choose sites aligned with your historical and cultural preferences.

2. **Itinerary Mapping:**

- **Sequential Order:** Plan a logical sequence for efficient exploration.

- **Time Allocation:** Allocate sufficient time for each site based on historical significance.

10.4.2 Interpreting Heritage Maps

1. **Key Symbols:**

- **Monuments:** Recognize symbols representing historical monuments.

- **Museums and Exhibits:** Identify icons denoting cultural institutions.

2. **Navigation Aids:** - **Directional Arrows:** Follow arrows for suggested routes within sites.

- **Information Points:** Locate areas with detailed historical information.

10.4.3 Navigating Historical Districts

1. **Street Layouts:**

- **Old Towns and Quarters:** Understand the structure of historical districts.

- **Cobblestone Roads:** Recognize traditional road surfaces in heritage areas.

2. **Landmark Identification:**

- **Building Features:** Differentiate architectural styles for landmark identification.

- **Plaza and Square Navigation:** Identify central gathering points within historical districts.

10.4.4 Preservation and Restoration

1. **Conservation Zones:**

- **Restricted Areas:** Respect zones under preservation and restoration.

- **Interactive Preservation:** Understand ongoing efforts to maintain cultural heritage.

2. **Heritage Trails:**

- **Themed Trails:** Explore curated paths highlighting specific historical themes.

- **Trail Markers:** Follow trail markers to stay on designated heritage routes.

10.4.5 Practical Tips

- Utilize audio guides or mobile apps for informative commentary during your tour. - Respect local regulations and cultural sensitivities while exploring heritage sites. - Engage with local guides for deeper insights into the history and culture of the area.

Immerse yourself in the richness of cultural and historical exploration, navigating through the past with precision. Whether it's ancient ruins, iconic landmarks, or centuries-old streets, make the most of your heritage tour with efficient and enjoyable navigation.

10.5 Preserving Cultural Landscapes

Delve into the art of preserving cultural landscapes – a concise guide to safeguarding the heritage and historical richness embedded in our surroundings.

10.5.1 Understanding Cultural Landscapes

1. **Definition and Significance:**

- **Cultural Layers:** Recognize the layers of history imprinted on landscapes.

- **Identity and Memory:** Understand how landscapes reflect cultural identity and memory.

2. **Types of Cultural Landscapes:**

- **Urban Heritage Zones:** Explore historic districts within modern urban settings.

- **Rural Cultural Landscapes:** Appreciate the cultural significance of rural areas.

10.5.2   Challenges and Threats

1. **Urbanization Impact:**

- **Infrastructure Development:** Assess the impact of new structures on cultural landscapes.

- **Population Growth:** Understand challenges posed by increasing urban populations.

2. **Environmental Factors:**

- **Natural Disasters:** Plan for preservation amid the threat of natural calamities.

- **Climate Change:** Address the impact of climate change on cultural sites.

10.5.3   Preservation Techniques

1. **Conservation Planning:**

- **Heritage Assessments:** Conduct assessments to determine preservation needs.

- **Zoning and Regulations:** Implement regulations to protect cultural landscapes.

2. **Sustainable Practices:**

- **Eco-friendly Restoration:** Integrate environmentally sustainable restoration practices.

- **Community Involvement:** Engage local communities in the preservation process.

10.5.4   Digital Preservation Tools

1. **GIS and Mapping:**

- **Digital Documentation:** Use GIS for comprehensive mapping and documentation.

- **Virtual Heritage Platforms:** Preserve landscapes digitally for future generations.

2. **Augmented Reality Applications:**

- **Historical Overlays:** Create augmented reality experiences to showcase historical landscapes.

- **Public Awareness:** Utilize AR to raise awareness about the importance of cultural preservation.

10.5.5   Cultural Landscape Management

1. **Interpretation Centers:**

- **Visitor Education:** Establish interpretation centers for visitor education.

- **Interactive Exhibits:** Use exhibits to convey the cultural significance of landscapes.

2. **Maintenance and Restoration:**

- **Periodic Maintenance:** Schedule regular maintenance to prevent deterioration.

- **Restoration Projects:** Undertake restoration projects with respect for historical authenticity.

10.5.6 Practical Tips

- Support local initiatives and organizations dedicated to cultural landscape preservation. - Advocate for responsible tourism practices to minimize the impact on cultural sites. - Stay informed about ongoing preservation efforts and contribute to community awareness.

Preserving cultural landscapes is not just a responsibility; it's a commitment to ensuring that the rich tapestry of our shared history remains intact for generations to come. Dive into the practical aspects of cultural landscape preservation and become a guardian of our collective heritage.

10.6 Map Reading in Archaeology

Embark on an archaeological journey through the lens of map reading – a swift guide to decoding the secrets of the past with practical insights and real-world applications.

10.6.1 Archaeological Mapping Basics

1. **Site Surveys:**

- **Grid Systems:** Understand the use of grid systems in archaeological site mapping.

- **Topographic Mapping:** Create detailed topographic maps for excavation planning.

2. **Recording Finds:**

- **Artifact Mapping:** Utilize maps to record the precise location of discovered artifacts.

- **Feature Mapping:** Document features such as structures and layers with accuracy.

10.6.2 Stratigraphy and Excavation Planning

1. **Understanding Stratigraphy:**

- **Stratigraphic Layers:** Interpret the chronological sequence of layers in excavation.

- **Harris Matrix:** Use the Harris Matrix to illustrate stratigraphic relationships.

2. **Excavation Grids:**

- **Establishing Grids:** Implement grids for systematic excavation and documentation.

- **Three-Dimensional Mapping:** Visualize excavation areas in three-dimensional space.

10.6.3   Geophysical Survey Mapping

1. **Ground Penetrating Radar (GPR):**

- **Principles of GPR:** Grasp the basics of GPR for subsurface feature detection.

- **Interpreting GPR Maps:** Decode GPR maps to identify potential archaeological features.

2. **Magnetic Surveys:**

- **Magnetic Anomalies:** Understand how magnetic anomalies indicate subsurface features.

- **Integration with Maps:** Integrate magnetic survey data with maps for comprehensive analysis.

10.6.4   GIS Applications in Archaeology

1. **Digital Site Recording:**

- **Database Integration:** Utilize GIS for the digital recording and storage of archaeological data.

- **Querying and Analysis:** Perform spatial queries and analysis for data interpretation.

2. **Remote Sensing in Archaeology:**

- **Aerial Photography:** Analyze aerial photographs for site identification and mapping.

- **LiDAR Technology:** Explore the applications of LiDAR in uncovering hidden archaeological features.

10.6.5   Mapping Artifacts and Features

1. **Artifact Cataloging:**

- **Digital Artifact Mapping:** Use GIS to create digital catalogs of artifacts.

- **Chronological Mapping:** Map artifacts based on their chronological context.

2. **Feature Mapping Techniques:**

- **Plan View Mapping:** Create plan view maps of architectural features.

- **Sectional Profiles:** Develop sectional profiles to visualize vertical features.

10.6.6   Practical Tips

- Collaborate with archaeologists and utilize their expertise in interpreting maps.

- Stay updated on advancements in archaeological mapping technologies.

- Foster a holistic understanding by combining map reading with on-site exploration.

Unearth the mysteries of the past with the practical application of map reading in archaeology. Navigate through time and space, decoding the stories written in the landscapes and artifacts of ancient civilizations.

Chapter 11

Educational Applications of Map Reading

11.1 Teaching Map Skills to Children

Embark on an engaging journey of teaching map skills to children – a vibrant exploration of educational techniques that make map reading a delightful and enriching experience for young minds.

11.1.1 Interactive Map Activities

1. **Treasure Hunt Adventures:**

- **Introduction to Coordinates:** Teach basic grid coordinates through treasure hunts.

- **Map Marking Techniques:** Encourage children to mark locations on their maps.

2. **Nature Exploration Maps:**

- **Outdoor Exploration:** Create maps for nature walks, parks, or school grounds.

- **Observation Skills:** Develop keen observation skills through map-based scavenger hunts.

11.1.2 Map Making and Drawing

1. **Personalized Treasure Maps:**

- **Creative Expression:** Allow children to design their own imaginary treasure maps.

- **Storytelling with Maps:** Encourage storytelling as children share the adventures on their maps.

2. **Community Maps:**

- **Collaborative Projects:** Engage in group projects to create maps of the local community.

- **Interviews and Surveys:** Integrate real-world elements by gathering information from community members.

11.1.3   Digital Map Tools for Kids

1. **Interactive Online Platforms:**

- **Kid-Friendly Apps:** Explore apps that gamify map reading for interactive learning.

- **Virtual Tours:** Take virtual trips using online maps to enhance geographical understanding.

2. **Educational Games:**

- **Map Puzzles:** Introduce puzzle games that involve assembling maps.

- **Geography Quiz Apps:** Foster friendly competition through geography quizzes.

11.1.4   Story Maps and Narratives

1. **Map-Integrated Storytelling:**

- **Book Reading with Maps:** Choose children's books with maps and integrate them into storytelling.

- **Map-Driven Narratives:** Create stories where characters navigate through illustrated maps.

2. **Historical and Fantasy Maps:** - **Time-Travel Maps:** Explore historical events or fantasy worlds through themed maps.

- **Class Projects:** Encourage map-based storytelling as part of classroom projects.

11.1.5   Practical Tips for Teachers and Parents

- Foster a positive attitude towards map reading by making it a fun and interactive experience.

- Incorporate map activities into other subjects like science, history, and arts for a multidisciplinary approach.

- Use colorful visuals, simple symbols, and relatable examples to simplify map concepts for children. Teaching map skills to children goes beyond cartography; it's an exciting journey that cultivates spatial awareness, curiosity, and a lifelong love for exploration. Make map reading a joyous adventure for the young learners!

11.2 Map Reading in Schools

Explore the dynamic integration of map reading into school curricula, transforming traditional learning into an interactive and engaging experience.

11.2.1 Geography Curriculum Enhancement

1. **Geography Games:**
- **Map-Based Board Games:** Introduce games that promote spatial awareness and geographical knowledge.
- **Geography Quiz Competitions:** Organize friendly competitions to reinforce map-related concepts.
2. **Field Trips and Map Exploration:**
- **Local Excursions:** Utilize local maps for field trips, fostering hands-on experience.
- **Map Challenges:** Create map-related challenges during field trips to enhance navigation skills.

11.2.2 Mathematics and Cartography Fusion

1. **Scale and Proportions:**
- **Mathematical Formulas:** Teach students how scale is represented mathematically on maps.
- **Practical Scale Exercises:** Engage in activities where students create maps with specified scales.
2. **Coordinates and Geometry:**
- **Introduction to Cartesian Coordinates:** Apply mathematical coordinates to map reading.
- **Geometric Shapes on Maps:** Explore the connection between geometry and map features.

11.2.3 History and Social Studies Integration

1. **Historical Map Analysis:**
- **Primary Source Exploration:** Study historical maps as primary sources for historical events.
- **Map Evolution:** Trace the changes in maps over different historical periods.
2. **Cultural Mapping Projects:**
- **Community Cultural Mapping:** Have students create maps reflecting the cultural diversity of their communities.
- **Historical Journey Maps:** Plot historical journeys of explorers or important figures on maps.

11.2.4 STEM Initiatives with Maps

1. **GIS and Data Mapping:**

- **Introduction to GIS:** Explore Geographic Information Systems for data mapping.

- **Student Data Projects:** Implement projects where students collect and map data.

2. **Environmental Studies:**

- **Mapping Environmental Changes:** Monitor environmental changes using maps.

- **Eco-Mapping:** Create maps highlighting ecological features and environmental concerns.

11.2.5 Innovative Map-Based Projects

1. **Augmented Reality Map Projects:**

- **AR Enhanced Maps:** Integrate augmented reality elements into map projects.

- **Virtual Tours:** Create virtual tours using AR for interactive learning experiences.

2. **Student-Driven Mapping Initiatives:**

- **Community Mapping:** Encourage students to map community resources and challenges.

- **Student Atlas Projects:** Collaborate on creating a school-specific atlas with student-contributed maps.

Map reading becomes a dynamic and multidisciplinary tool in schools, fostering a holistic approach to education that combines geography, mathematics, history, and technology. Embrace the transformative power of maps in shaping well-rounded learners!

11.3 Outdoor Education with Maps

Embarking on a journey of outdoor education with maps opens up a world of hands-on learning experiences that blend exploration, navigation, and environmental appreciation. Here, we delve into practical and engaging methods for incorporating map reading into outdoor education.

11.3.1 Nature Mapping Adventures

1. **Trail Mapping Expeditions:**

- **Introduction to Topography:** Explore local trails, parks, or natural areas.

- **Elevation Changes:** Demonstrate contour lines and elevation with hands-on examples.

2. **Botanical Mapping:**

- **Identifying Flora:** Use maps to mark locations of various plant species.

- **Creating Field Guides:** Compile a field guide based on observed plant life.

11.3.2 Survival Skills and Navigation

1. **Orienteering Challenges:** - **Map and Compass Navigation:** Teach basic orienteering skills.
- **Wayfinding Techniques:** Introduce natural indicators for direction.
2. **Shelter Building and Mapping:** - **Map-Integrated Shelter Design:** Plan and build shelters using map references. - **Emergency Navigation:** Teach navigation in challenging outdoor scenarios.

11.3.3 Geocaching Adventures

1. **Geocaching Basics:**
- **Introduction to GPS Coordinates:** Combine technology with map-based treasure hunting.
- **Creating Geocache Maps:** Design treasure maps for geocaching adventures.
2. **Geological Mapping:**
- **Rock and Mineral Exploration:** Map locations of interesting geological features.
- **Landform Recognition:** Learn to identify landforms using maps.

11.3.4 Environmental Studies with Maps

1. **Watershed Mapping:** - **Understanding Watersheds:** Explore the concept of watersheds on local maps.
- **Water Quality Mapping:** Monitor and map water quality in different locations.
2. **Wildlife Observation Maps:**
- **Identifying Habitats:** Use maps to locate and observe wildlife habitats.
- **Migration Patterns:** Study seasonal migration routes on maps.

11.3.5 Practical Tips for Outdoor Map Education

- Incorporate map reading into outdoor activities to reinforce theoretical concepts.
- Use map-related games and challenges to keep the learning experience enjoyable.
- Encourage collaborative map projects that foster teamwork and communication skills.
- Link map reading to environmental stewardship to instill a sense of responsibility.

Outdoor education with maps not only enhances navigational skills but also nurtures a deep connection with the natural world. Make outdoor map adventures a cornerstone of experiential learning for students!

11.4　Integrating Geography and Cartography

In this section, we explore innovative ways to seamlessly integrate geography and cartography into educational settings, creating dynamic learning experiences that captivate students' interest and enhance their map reading skills.

11.4.1　Geographical Games and Challenges

1. **Map-Based Scavenger Hunts:**

- **Geographical Clues:** Develop clues based on map coordinates and landmarks.

- **Team Exploration:** Foster teamwork as students navigate the scavenger hunt.

2. **Geographical Puzzles:**

- **Landform Jigsaw Puzzles:** Create puzzles to assemble geographical features.

- **Map Puzzle Competitions:** Engage students in friendly competitions.

11.4.2　Interactive Mapping Projects

1. **Historical Geography Projects:**

- **Time Travel Maps:** Develop maps showcasing historical changes in geography.

- **Storytelling through Maps:** Encourage students to narrate historical events using maps.

2. **Cultural Cartography:**

- **Mapping Cultural Influences:** Illustrate the impact of culture on geographical landscapes.

- **Customized Cultural Maps:** Create personalized maps reflecting students' cultural backgrounds.

11.4.3　Mathematical Elements in Cartography

1. **Scale and Proportions:**

- **Scale Calculations:** Explore mathematical formulas for map scaling.

- **Proportional Representation:** Understand how map elements reflect real-world proportions.

2. **Statistical Mapping:**

- **Population Density Maps:** Integrate statistical data into map representations.

- **Economic Indicator Maps:** Illustrate economic trends through cartography.

11.4.4   Field Trips and Map Exploration

1. **Outdoor Geography Trails:**

- **Field Trips with Maps:** Plan excursions incorporating map reading activities.

- **Natural Geography Observations:** Connect theoretical concepts with real-world geography.

2. **Map-Enhanced Virtual Tours:**

- **Google Earth Expeditions:** Explore virtual maps for global geography.

- **Interactive Virtual Maps:** Customize virtual tours for specific educational themes.

11.4.5   Practical Tips for Integration

- Utilize digital mapping tools to enhance engagement and interactive learning.

- Encourage students to create their maps for specific projects or presentations.

- Integrate map reading into interdisciplinary subjects for a holistic educational experience.

- Emphasize the real-world applications of geography and cartography in various professions.

By seamlessly blending geography and cartography, educators can transform map reading into a dynamic and interdisciplinary learning adventure, fostering a deeper understanding of the world.

11.5   Map Challenges and Competitions

Elevate the excitement of map reading in educational settings by introducing map challenges and competitions. Engage students in dynamic learning experiences that foster teamwork, critical thinking, and a passion for cartography.

11.5.1   Treasure Hunt Extravaganza

1. **Map-Based Treasure Hunt:**

- **Coordinate Calculations:** Teach students how to interpret and use coordinates.

- **Treasure Map Creation:** Encourage students to design their own treasure maps.

2. **Geocaching Competitions:**

- **Introduction to Geocaching:** Explain the principles of geocaching using maps.

- **Team Challenges:** Organize geocaching competitions with teams competing for hidden treasures.

11.5.2 Orienteering Olympics

1. **Map Relay Races:**

- **Map Handover Techniques:** Train students on efficient map handovers during relays.

- **Speed and Accuracy:** Emphasize the balance between speed and accurate navigation.

2. **Night Orienteering Challenge:**

- **Navigating in Low Light:** Introduce challenges of map reading in nighttime conditions.

- **Safety Protocols:** Teach students to use flashlights and navigate safely in the dark.

11.5.3 Map Puzzle Championships

1. **Topographic Puzzle Solving:**

- **Contour Line Puzzles:** Create puzzles based on contour lines for spatial understanding.

- **Speed Challenges:** Time students as they solve topographic map puzzles.

2. **Interactive Map Quizzes:**

- **Map Identification:** Conduct quizzes on identifying countries, landmarks, or geographical features.

- **Interactive Response Systems:** Use technology for real-time responses and engagement.

11.5.4 Inter-School Map Debates

1. **Geopolitical Map Debates:**

- **World Affairs Discussion:** Use geopolitical maps as a basis for informed discussions.

- **Current Events Integration:** Relate map debates to contemporary global issues.

2. **Historical Map Analysis:**

- **Analyzing Historical Borders:** Explore historical maps and discuss geopolitical changes.

- **Role-Playing Scenarios:** Encourage students to act out historical events using maps.

11.5.5 Practical Tips for Map Challenges

- Infuse a sense of fun and friendly competition to keep students motivated.

- Foster collaboration by organizing team-based challenges.

- Incorporate map challenges into broader subjects for interdisciplinary learning.

- Recognize and reward creativity and innovative map solutions.

Map challenges and competitions turn map reading into an exhilarating educational journey, inspiring students to become adept navigators and geographers.

11.6 Life-Long Learning in Map Mastery

Embark on a life-long journey of map mastery, fostering a continuous learning mindset for individuals of all ages. Explore practical approaches, real-world applications, and the joy of discovering the world through maps.

11.6.1 Everyday Map Integration

1. **Commute Planning:**
- **Optimizing Routes:** Utilize maps to plan efficient daily commutes.
- **Real-Time Traffic Updates:** Integrate real-time data for dynamic route adjustments.
2. **Travel Adventures:**
- **Adventure Planning:** Plan vacations and explore new destinations using maps.
- **Cultural Exploration:** Learn about local cultures and landmarks through maps.

11.6.2 Navigating the Digital Landscape

1. **Digital Map Applications:**
- **Smartphone Navigation:** Embrace digital map apps for real-time guidance.
- **Augmented Reality Exploration:** Use AR features to enhance map interactions.
2. **Virtual Travel Experiences:**
- **Virtual Tours:** Explore historical and cultural sites virtually through digital maps.
- **Interactive Learning Platforms:** Engage with educational content using map-based platforms.

11.6.3 Environmental Awareness

1. **Ecological Mapping:**
- **Biodiversity Maps:** Understand and contribute to biodiversity mapping efforts.

- **Environmental Impact Assessment:** Assess the environmental impact of human activities.

2. **Weather Mapping:**

- **Meteorological Understanding:** Learn to interpret weather maps for better forecasting.

- **Emergency Preparedness:** Use weather maps for disaster preparedness.

11.6.4   Personal Development Through Map Challenges

1. **Fitness Tracking:**

- **Hiking and Running Routes:** Plan and track fitness activities with map apps.

- **Competitive Challenges:** Join map-based fitness challenges for motivation.

2. **Culinary Exploration:**

- **Ingredient Sourcing:** Understand the geographical origin of food ingredients.

- **Global Culinary Tours:** Explore diverse cuisines through map-guided culinary adventures.

11.6.5   Continuous Skill Enhancement

1. **Advanced Navigation Courses:**

- **Online Learning Platforms:** Enroll in courses for advanced map reading skills.

- **Professional Certification:** Pursue certifications to enhance map-related expertise.

2. **Community Engagement:**

- **Map-Related Clubs and Meetups:** Join local or online groups for shared learning experiences.

- **Map-athon Events:** Participate in map-related community events and contribute to mapping projects.

11.6.6   Practical Tips for Life-Long Learning

- Emphasize the practical utility of maps in everyday scenarios.

- Encourage curiosity and exploration through diverse map applications.

- Foster a sense of adventure and discovery in map-based activities.

- Leverage digital tools and platforms for continuous map education.

Life-long learning in map mastery transforms the act of reading maps into a dynamic and enriching journey, contributing to personal growth and a deeper understanding of the world.

Chapter 12

Environmental Awareness through Maps

12.1 Mapping Climate Change

Uncover the intricate world of climate change through the lens of maps, making environmental awareness accessible and engaging.

12.1.1 Understanding Climate Data

1. **Temperature Patterns:**

- **Global Temperature Maps:** Visualize temperature variations worldwide.

- **Time-lapse Analysis:** Observe changes in temperature over specific periods.

2. **Precipitation Trends:**

- **Rainfall and Drought Maps:** Explore regions experiencing water abundance or scarcity.

- **Seasonal Variations:** Understand how precipitation patterns evolve with seasons.

12.1.2 Oceanic and Atmospheric Mapping

1. **Ocean Currents:**

- **Current Flow Maps:** Track the movement of ocean currents globally.

- **Impact on Climate:** Understand how ocean currents influence local and global climates.

2. **Air Circulation Patterns:**

- **Jet Stream Mapping:** Study the high-altitude winds impacting weather patterns.

- **Climate Zones:** Explore how air circulation contributes to diverse climate zones.

12.1.3   GIS Applications in Climate Research

1. **Mapping Greenhouse Gas Emissions:**

- **Emission Source Identification:** Pinpoint major sources of greenhouse gases.

- **Impact on Global Warming:** Visualize the correlation between emissions and rising temperatures.

2. **Deforestation Mapping:**

- **Loss of Forest Cover:** Track deforestation trends through satellite imagery.

- **Biodiversity Impact:** Understand the ecological consequences of deforestation.

12.1.4   Real-time Environmental Monitoring

1. **Wildfire Tracking:**

- **Fire Incident Maps:** Monitor active wildfires and their progression.

- **Preventive Measures:** Plan and implement strategies for wildfire prevention.

2. **Air Quality Mapping:**

- **Pollution Hotspots:** Identify areas with high levels of air pollution.

- **Health Impacts:** Understand the health implications of poor air quality.

12.1.5   Community Involvement in Climate Mapping

1. **Citizen Science Projects:**

- **Crowdsourced Data Collection:** Engage communities in gathering climate-related data.

- **Localized Impact:** Showcase how individual contributions can drive change.

2. **Mapping Climate Resilience:**

- **Vulnerability Maps:** Identify regions at risk due to climate change.

- **Adaptation Strategies:** Highlight initiatives and strategies for building climate resilience.

12.1.6   Practical Tips for Environmental Engagement

- Promote the accessibility of climate data through user-friendly maps.

- Encourage active participation in citizen science projects for real-world impact.

- Demonstrate the interconnectedness of climate factors through visually compelling maps.

- Foster a sense of responsibility by showcasing the role individuals play in environmental stewardship.

Mapping climate change is not just a scientific endeavor but a call to action, empowering individuals to be stewards of the planet's health.

12.2　Conservation Mapping

Embark on a journey into conservation mapping, where the power of maps is harnessed to protect and preserve our planet's biodiversity.

12.2.1　Mapping Biodiversity Hotspots

1. **Identification of Hotspots:**

- **Species Diversity Maps:** Visualize regions with high biodiversity.

- **Endangered Species Focus:** Highlight areas crucial for endangered species conservation.

2. **Habitat Mapping:**

- **Ecosystem Distribution:** Map the diverse habitats supporting various species.

- **Fragmentation Analysis:** Identify areas at risk due to habitat fragmentation.

12.2.2　GIS Applications for Conservation

1. **Wildlife Corridor Mapping:**

- **Connectivity Maps:** Illustrate corridors promoting wildlife movement.

- **Impact on Migration:** Understand the importance of corridors in seasonal migrations.

2. **Protected Area Management:**

- **Zoning for Conservation:** Map zones within protected areas for specific conservation purposes.

- **Human-Wildlife Conflict Areas:** Highlight regions where conservation efforts intersect with human activities.

12.2.3　Mapping Threats to Biodiversity

1. **Deforestation Impact Maps:**

- **Loss of Biodiversity:** Visualize the consequences of deforestation on ecosystems.

- **Reforestation Opportunities:** Identify areas for potential restoration efforts.

2. **Climate Change Vulnerability:**

- **Species at Risk:** Map the vulnerability of different species to climate change.

- **Adaptation Strategies:** Suggest conservation strategies based on climate vulnerability.

12.2.4   Real-time Conservation Monitoring

1. **Poaching Incidents:**

- **Incident Heat Maps:** Monitor and respond to poaching incidents in real-time.

- **Patrol Route Optimization:** Optimize patrol routes for maximum conservation impact.

2. **Invasive Species Tracking:**

- **Spread Maps:** Monitor the spread of invasive species affecting local ecosystems.

- **Eradication Planning:** Plan targeted interventions for invasive species management.

12.2.5   Community Involvement in Conservation Mapping

1. **Citizen Science Initiatives:**

- **Biodiversity Data Collection:** Engage communities in monitoring local biodiversity.

- **Conservation Education:** Promote awareness and understanding of local conservation efforts.

2. **Mapping Restoration Projects:**

- **Community-led Restoration Maps:** Showcase projects led by local communities.

- **Economic and Ecological Benefits:** Highlight the positive impacts of restoration efforts.

12.2.6   Practical Tips for Conservation Mapping

- Emphasize the role of local communities in biodiversity conservation through participatory mapping.

- Utilize GIS technologies for real-time monitoring of conservation initiatives.

- Showcase the interconnectedness of various species and ecosystems through visually impactful maps.

- Advocate for the importance of conservation mapping in preserving the planet's rich biodiversity. Conservation mapping is a dynamic tool that empowers communities and organizations to safeguard the Earth's biodiversity for future generations.

12.3 Wildlife Tracking and Mapping

Embark on an exciting journey into the world of wildlife tracking and mapping, where cutting-edge technologies meet the wonders of the animal kingdom.

12.3.1 Introduction to Wildlife Tracking

1. **GPS Collars for Animal Monitoring:**

- **Real-time Location Data:** Track animals in real-time using GPS technology.

- **Behavioral Insights:** Understand animal behavior through movement patterns.

2. **Satellite Tagging for Marine Species:**

- **Oceanic Migration Routes:** Map the incredible journeys of marine species.

- **Conservation of Endangered Species:** Focus on species vulnerable to overfishing.

12.3.2 Mathematics Behind Wildlife Mapping

1. **Trilateration in GPS Tracking:**

- **Determining Animal Position:** Explore the mathematical concept of trilateration.

- **Error Reduction Techniques:** Enhance accuracy in tracking calculations.

2. **Predictive Modeling for Animal Movements:**

- **Markov Chain Models:** Predict future locations based on historical movement.

- **Habitat Utilization Probability:** Assess the likelihood of animals occupying specific areas.

12.3.3 Mapping Animal Migration Patterns

1. **Dynamic Range Mapping:**

- **Seasonal Movement Maps:** Visualize the dynamic ranges animals explore.

- **Climate Influence on Migration:** Understand how climate impacts migration patterns.

2. **GIS Applications in Wildlife Tracking:**

- **Corridor Mapping:** Identify critical migration corridors for conservation.

- **Human-Wildlife Conflict Prevention:** Analyze areas prone to conflicts for proactive measures.

12.3.4 Conservation Strategies Based on Tracking Data

1. **Protected Area Design Using Animal Movements:**

- **Optimal Reserve Placement:** Map areas critical for preserving animal habitats.

- **Corridor Creation:** Enhance connectivity between protected areas.

2. **Mitigating Human-Wildlife Conflict:**

- **Mapping Conflict Hotspots:** Identify areas where human activities intersect with wildlife.

- **Community Engagement:** Involve local communities in conflict resolution strategies.

12.3.5 Technological Advances in Wildlife Mapping

1. **Drone Technology for Aerial Surveys:**

- **Population Density Estimation:** Utilize drones for wildlife population studies.

- **Illegal Activity Detection:** Monitor for poaching activities from the air.

2. **Machine Learning in Wildlife Tracking:**

- **Behavioral Pattern Recognition:** Train models to recognize specific animal behaviors.

- **Early Warning Systems:** Predict potential threats to wildlife based on machine learning insights.

12.3.6 Educational and Public Awareness Aspects

1. **Interactive Wildlife Maps for Education:**

- **Virtual Tours:** Bring wildlife habitats into classrooms through interactive maps.

- **Inspiring Future Conservationists:** Engage students in the wonders of wildlife tracking.

2. **Open Data Initiatives in Wildlife Mapping:**

- **Data Sharing for Conservation:** Encourage open data practices to support global conservation efforts.

- **Citizen Science Programs:** Involve the public in contributing to wildlife tracking datasets.

12.3.7 Practical Tips for Wildlife Tracking and Mapping

- Embrace interdisciplinary approaches, combining biology, technology, and mathematics for comprehensive wildlife mapping.

- Advocate for the ethical use of tracking technologies, prioritizing animal welfare and conservation goals.

- Utilize tracking data not only for research but also for fostering public awareness and involvement in wildlife conservation.

Wildlife tracking and mapping offer a fascinating lens into the lives of animals, providing valuable insights for conservation and coexistence.

12.4 Environmental Impact Assessment

Embark on a journey to understand the crucial role of environmental impact assessment (EIA) and how maps play a pivotal role in evaluating and mitigating the impact of human activities on the environment.

12.4.1 Understanding Environmental Impact Assessment

1. **Purpose of EIA:**
- **Predicting Environmental Consequences:** Use maps to foresee the impacts of projects on ecosystems.
- **Decision-Making Tool:** Aid in making informed choices balancing development and environmental conservation.
2. **Stages of EIA:**
- **Scoping:** Identify the key issues and boundaries of the assessment area using maps.
- **Impact Analysis:** Visualize and quantify potential impacts on the environment through mapping.

12.4.2 Mapping Techniques in EIA

1. **GIS Applications in Impact Mapping:**
- **Overlay Analysis:** Identify areas where project activities overlap with sensitive ecosystems.
- **Buffer Analysis:** Evaluate the spatial extent of potential impacts around project sites.
2. **Remote Sensing for Environmental Monitoring:**
- **Satellite Imagery:** Monitor changes in land use and vegetation cover over time.
- **Change Detection Maps:** Highlight alterations in the environment caused by human activities.

12.4.3 Mathematics and Formulas in EIA

1. **Calculating Environmental Indices:**
- **Biodiversity Index:** Assess the richness of species in an area affected by a project.

- **Air Quality Index:** Quantify the impact on air quality due to industrial activities.

2. **Risk Assessment Formulas:**

- **Ecological Risk Assessment:** Evaluate the potential harm to ecosystems using mathematical models.

- **Human Health Risk Assessment:** Quantify the risks posed to human populations from environmental changes.

12.4.4   Case Studies and Practical Applications

1. **EIA in Urban Development:**

- **Infrastructure Projects:** Assess the impact of urban development on local ecosystems.

- **Transportation Planning:** Analyze the environmental consequences of new transportation routes.

2. **Natural Resource Extraction EIA:**

- **Mining Impact Mapping:** Visualize the disturbance caused by mining activities on landscapes.

- **Oil and Gas Exploration:** Evaluate the ecological footprint of extraction projects.

12.4.5   Community Involvement and Public Awareness

1. **Community Mapping in EIA:**

- **Participatory GIS:** Involve local communities in mapping potential impacts.

- **Environmental Justice Mapping:** Identify areas where vulnerable populations may be disproportionately affected.

2. **Public Awareness Campaigns:**

- **Visual Impact Assessments:** Use maps to communicate potential changes in the landscape to the public.

- **Accessible Map Formats:** Ensure maps are user-friendly for broader public engagement.

12.4.6   Future Trends in EIA Mapping

1. **Integration of AI in Impact Assessment:**

- **Predictive Modeling:** Utilize artificial intelligence for more accurate predictions of environmental impacts.

- **Automated Monitoring Systems:** Implement AI-driven systems for continuous environmental monitoring.

2. **Global Collaboration in EIA:**

- **Shared Databases:** Promote international cooperation by sharing environmental impact data.

- **Unified Standards:** Work towards standardized methodologies for conducting EIAs globally.

Environmental Impact Assessment through maps serves as a powerful tool for balancing human development with environmental preservation.

12.5 Participatory Mapping

Discover the dynamic world of participatory mapping, a powerful approach to engage communities in environmental awareness and decision-making.

12.5.1 What is Participatory Mapping?

1. **Community Empowerment:**

- **Inclusive Decision-Making:** Engage local communities in mapping to ensure their voices are heard.

- **Collaborative Data Creation:** Foster a sense of ownership and responsibility for local environmental issues.

2. **Tools for Participatory Mapping:**

- **Hand-drawn Maps:** Simple yet effective tools for expressing local knowledge.

- **Digital Platforms:** Leverage user-friendly apps and software for collaborative mapping.

12.5.2 Steps in Conducting Participatory Mapping

1. **Community Engagement:**

- **Workshops and Meetings:** Facilitate gatherings to introduce the concept of mapping.

- **Local Knowledge Sharing:** Encourage community members to share their insights about the environment.

2. **Mapping Techniques:**

- **Land Use Mapping:** Identify areas used for agriculture, housing, or cultural purposes.

- **Resource Mapping:** Pinpoint valuable environmental resources and potential threats.

12.5.3   Mathematics and Formulas in Participatory Mapping

1. **Spatial Analysis for Decision-Making:**

- **Proximity Analysis:** Assess the spatial relationships between community resources and potential hazards.

- **Community Accessibility Index:** Quantify the ease with which community members can access essential resources.

2. **Community-Based Monitoring Metrics:**

- **Participation Rate:** Calculate the percentage of community members actively involved in mapping.

- **Spatial Discrepancy Index:** Evaluate variations in the perception of environmental issues among community members.

12.5.4   Real-world Applications of Participatory Mapping

1. **Natural Resource Management:**

- **Forest Conservation:** Engage local communities in mapping to monitor and protect forested areas.

- **Water Resource Mapping:** Identify water sources and track changes in water quality.

2. **Disaster Preparedness and Response:**

- **Vulnerability Mapping:** Assess the susceptibility of communities to natural disasters.

- **Emergency Evacuation Plans:** Collaboratively develop evacuation routes and safe zones.

12.5.5   Challenges and Solutions in Participatory Mapping

1. **Technological Barriers:**

- **Digital Literacy Workshops:** Address technological challenges through training sessions.

- **Accessible Mapping Tools:** Choose platforms that are user-friendly and require minimal technical expertise.

2. **Data Accuracy and Validation:**

- **Community Validation Sessions:** Organize community meetings to review and validate the accuracy of the mapped information.

- **Collaborative Data Verification:** Engage multiple community members in cross-checking and validating data.

12.5.6 Future Trends in Participatory Mapping

1. **Virtual Reality Integration:**
- **Immersive Mapping Experiences:** Explore the use of virtual reality to enhance participatory mapping experiences.
- **Remote Participation:** Allow community members to contribute virtually to mapping initiatives.
2. **Global Networks of Collaboration:**
- **Shared Participatory Platforms:** Establish interconnected platforms for communities worldwide to share experiences.
- **Common Mapping Standards:** Develop standardized protocols for participatory mapping to ensure consistency.

Participatory mapping empowers communities to become active contributors to environmental awareness, fostering a sense of shared responsibility and collective action.

12.6 Promoting Eco-Friendly Navigation

Embark on a journey towards sustainable navigation practices and environmental consciousness.

12.6.1 Eco-Friendly Navigation Practices

1. **Efficient Route Planning:**
- **Optimal Pathfinding Algorithms:** Utilize algorithms to find the most fuel-efficient routes.
- **Emission Reduction Models:** Estimate carbon emissions for different routes and choose eco-friendly options.
2. **Renewable Energy Integration:**
- **Solar-Powered Navigation Systems:** Implement solar panels to generate energy for navigation equipment.
- **Wind-Powered Solutions:** Explore innovative wind-assisted propulsion technologies for eco-friendly vessels.

12.6.2 Mathematics in Eco-Friendly Navigation

1. **Fuel Consumption Calculations:**

- **Fuel Efficiency Equations:** Determine fuel consumption based on vessel speed and load.

- **Carbon Emission Formulas:** Quantify carbon emissions using mathematical models.

2. **Optimizing Speed for Efficiency:**

- **Speed-Fuel Consumption Curves:** Analyze the relationship between vessel speed and fuel efficiency.

- **Economic Speed Calculations:** Find the speed that minimizes fuel consumption and environmental impact.

12.6.3 Real-world Applications and Case Studies

1. **Green Ports and Harbors:**

- **Renewable Energy Infrastructure:** Implement solar and wind energy solutions in port facilities.

- **Electric Shore Power:** Offer electric power to docked vessels to reduce onboard generator use.

2. **Incentivizing Sustainable Practices:**

- **Eco-Friendly Certification:** Introduce certifications for vessels adhering to environmentally conscious practices.

- **Financial Incentives:** Provide economic benefits for ships using eco-friendly technologies and practices.

12.6.4 Challenges and Solutions in Eco-Friendly Navigation

1. **Technological Barriers:**

- **Research and Development Funding:** Invest in R&D to overcome technological hurdles.

- **Public-Private Collaboration:** Foster partnerships to accelerate the development of green navigation technologies.

2. **Resistance to Change:**

- **Awareness Campaigns:** Educate stakeholders about the environmental impact of navigation practices.

- **Policy Advocacy:** Lobby for regulations promoting eco-friendly navigation on a global scale.

12.6.5 Future Trends in Eco-Friendly Navigation

1. **Autonomous and Electric Vessels:**

- **Green Autonomous Fleets:** Develop self-sustaining, electrically powered autonomous vessels.

- **Battery Technology Advancements:** Explore cutting-edge battery technologies for electric maritime propulsion.

2. **Smart Navigation Systems:**

- **AI-driven Efficiency Optimization:** Implement artificial intelligence to continuously optimize navigation routes.

- **Dynamic Emission Monitoring:** Integrate real-time emission monitoring systems for immediate feedback.

Promoting eco-friendly navigation is not just a choice but a responsibility, fostering a sustainable and harmonious coexistence with our planet.

Chapter 13

Conclusion

13.1 Reviewing Your Map Reading Journey

As you conclude your map reading journey, reflect on the knowledge gained and the practical skills acquired.

13.1.1 Mathematics in Map Reading

1. **Understanding Scale:**
- **Scale Factor Formulas:** Recap the equations for converting map distances to real-world distances.
- **Ratio Calculations:** Apply the concept of ratios to interpret scale in various map types.
2. **Navigating with Coordinates:**
- **Latitude and Longitude Equations:** Revisit the formulas for converting coordinates between degrees, minutes, and seconds.
- **UTM Coordinate Systems:** Explore the mathematics behind Universal Transverse Mercator (UTM) coordinates.

13.1.2 Practical Map Reading Techniques

1. **Topographic Map Interpretation:**
- **Contour Line Mathematics:** Revisit contour interval calculations for elevation changes.
- **Gradient and Slope Calculations:** Understand the mathematics behind slope determination.

2. **Compass Navigation:**

- **Bearing Calculations:** Refresh your memory on calculating bearings between two points.

- **Triangulation Formulas:** Review the mathematical foundations of triangulating your position.

13.1.3   Advanced Navigation Technologies

1. **GPS Navigation:**

- **Trilateration Concepts:** Understand the mathematical principles behind GPS position determination.

- **Satellite Geometry Impact:** Explore how the arrangement of GPS satellites affects accuracy.

2. **GIS and Remote Sensing:**

- **Spatial Analysis Formulas:** Review mathematical methods for analyzing spatial data.

- **Radiometric Correction Equations:** Understand the correction processes in remote sensing.

13.1.4   Environmental and Cultural Awareness through Maps

1. **Eco-Friendly Navigation:**

- **Carbon Footprint Calculations:** Revisit methods for calculating and reducing carbon emissions in navigation.

- **Renewable Energy Integration:** Understand how renewable energy can be incorporated into maritime navigation.

2. **Cultural and Historical Maps:**

- **Interpreting Historical Maps:** Practice interpreting historical maps using a combination of historical context and cartographic elements.

- **Cultural Heritage Mapping:** Explore how mapping is used to preserve and promote cultural heritage.

As you review your map reading journey, remember that maps are not just paper with lines; they are gateways to understanding our world in all its complexity. Keep exploring, navigating, and discovering the wonders that maps unfold.

13.2   Practical Exercises and Applications

As you conclude your map reading journey, engage in practical exercises and applications to reinforce your skills.

13.2.1 Navigation Challenges

1. **Orienteering Adventure:**

- **Map and Compass Relay:** Create a relay race incorporating map reading and compass navigation skills.

- **Night Navigation Challenge:** Practice navigating using a compass in low-light conditions.

2. **GPS Geocaching:**

- **Geocaching Hunt:** Organize or participate in a geocaching event to apply GPS navigation skills.

- **Multi-Cache Exploration:** Challenge yourself with multi-caches that involve solving puzzles using coordinates.

13.2.2 Outdoor Survival Scenarios

1. **Emergency Shelter Building:**

- **Shelter Construction:** Demonstrate building emergency shelters using natural materials.

- **Weather-Resistant Designs:** Explore techniques for creating shelters that withstand different weather conditions.

2. **Natural Navigation Techniques:**

- **Sun and Stars Navigation:** Practice finding direction using the sun and stars without a compass.

- **Edible Plant Identification:** Learn to identify edible plants as a survival skill.

13.2.3 Environmental Mapping Projects

1. **Conservation Mapping:**

- **Local Conservation Project:** Develop a map outlining areas for conservation and environmental protection.

- **Biodiversity Mapping:** Map the distribution of plant and animal species in a specific area.

2. **Climate Change Impact Assessment:**

- **Temperature and Precipitation Trends:** Analyze historical climate data to assess local climate change impacts.

- **Sea Level Rise Mapping:** Use GIS tools to visualize potential sea level rise effects on coastal areas.

13.2.4 Educational Initiatives

1. **Map Reading Workshops:**

- **School Outreach Program:** Conduct map reading workshops for local schools to enhance geographic literacy.

- **Community Education Seminar:** Organize seminars on map reading and navigation for the community.

2. **Map Challenges and Competitions:**

- **Local Map Challenge:** Host a map reading competition to encourage community participation.

- **Youth Mapping Contest:** Initiate a contest for young individuals to showcase their map reading skills.

Engaging in these practical exercises and applications will not only solidify your map reading skills but also contribute to your ability to navigate, survive, and make a positive impact on your environment and community.

13.3 Continuing Your Map Mastery

As you conclude your map reading journey, consider the following steps to continue honing your skills in a practical and enjoyable manner:

13.3.1 Geocaching Adventures

1. **Advanced Geocaching:**

- **Puzzle Caches:** Challenge yourself with geocaches that involve deciphering puzzles and codes.

- **Mystery and Multi-Caches:** Explore caches that require solving multiple stages, enhancing your navigation prowess.

2. **Geocaching Events:**

- **Community Meetups:** Attend local geocaching events to connect with fellow enthusiasts and share experiences.

- **CITO (Cache In, Trash Out):** Participate in CITO events to contribute to environmental cleanliness while geocaching.

13.3.2   Advanced Navigation Techniques

1. **Celestial Navigation:**

- **Star and Planet Identification:** Learn to use stars and planets for navigation during both day and night.

- **Sun Compass:** Understand how to create an improvised compass using the sun's position.

2. **Wilderness Survival Skills:**

- **Edible Plant Foraging:** Expand your knowledge of edible plants to enhance your survival skills.

- **Water Sourcing and Purification:** Learn techniques for finding and purifying water in the wild.

13.3.3   Map Technology Integration

1. **GIS Projects:**

- **Custom Map Creation:** Dive into GIS software to create personalized maps tailored to your interests.

- **Overlay Analysis:** Explore overlaying different map layers for more comprehensive insights.

2. **Augmented Reality Exploration:**

- **AR Navigation Apps:** Experiment with augmented reality apps for navigation in urban and natural environments.

- **Map Overlays:** Implement AR overlays to enhance your understanding of real-world locations.

13.3.4   Educational Outreach

1. **Mentorship and Workshops:**

- **Map Reading Mentorship:** Mentor others in map reading skills to foster a sense of community.

- **Workshop Facilitation:** Conduct workshops for schools or community groups, sharing your expertise.

2. **Citizen Science Initiatives:**

- **Mapping for Citizen Science:** Contribute to citizen science projects involving mapping and environmental monitoring.

- **Collaborative Mapping:** Engage in collaborative mapping efforts for community development and awareness.

Continuing your map mastery involves staying curious, embracing challenges, and sharing your knowledge with others. Whether you're exploring advanced geocaching or delving into celestial navigation, the journey towards map mastery is an exciting and ongoing adventure.

www.ingramcontent.com/pod-product-compliance
Lightning Source LLC
Chambersburg PA
CBHW080853250726
48663CB00004B/448